WINNING LIKE SAINA

Jatin Gupta is the Head of Business Operations at a leading sports-related company. He is a management professional with over fourteen years of work experience in consumer product, consulting, financial services and sports industry. He has handled various leadership positions with different organizations like Deloitte and Invesco. A traveller at heart, Jatin is also a voracious reader who likes to indulge in the world of biographies and fiction often. This is his first attempt at non-fiction where he has tried to share few of his learning's from the professional world.

WINNING LIKE SAINA
THINK & SUCCEED LIKE NEHWAL

JATIN GUPTA

RUPA

Published by
Rupa Publications India Pvt. Ltd 2018
7/16, Ansari Road, Daryaganj
New Delhi 110002

Sales centres:
Allahabad Bengaluru Chennai
Hyderabad Jaipur Kathmandu
Kolkata Mumbai

ISBN: 978-93-5304-062-8

First impression 2018

10 9 8 7 6 5 4 3 2 1

Printed at Parksons Graphics Pvt.Ltd., Mumbai

Contents

Introduction

Saina Nehwal:

Poster Girl of Indian Badminton

> I'm not so talented. There are many, many players more talented than me. I just work very hard to stay at the top of my game.[1]
>
> —Saina Nehwal

It is humble statements like above which define Saina Nehwal, the first badminton superstar produced in India. In a cricket-crazy country like ours where even a small club level match can jostle up more crowd than any national-level

[1]https://www.sportskeeda.com/badminton/saina-nehwal-interview-bengaluru-2015

match of any other sport, Saina has turned the tides to gather crowds in appreciation of her craft and calibre.

Easily regarded as among the top ten sports celebrities in India, she has been conferred with Padma Bhushan (2016), the third highest civilian award in India.

In many ways she has been the flag-bearer of badminton in India who has marched the road on which we now see players like P.V. Sindhu, K. Srikanth, Prannoy H.S., Rituparna Das and B. Sai Praneeth walking gloriously.

I still remember the first time I read Saina's name, it was in a news article published by one of the leading dailies. I was pleasantly amazed by the twelve-year-old defeating players six to seven years older to her. There was a fair amount of wow in the way I read the news piece, very inspirational.

To say the least, Saina was a spark right from a very early age, she had the talent, will, attitude and most importantly a burning desire to win, which shaped her into the icon that she is.

From India Open to Olympics, she has made her mark in all the major badminton arenas. Every time she walks to the centre of the court her individual accolades are overtaken by her deep desire to hold the Indian Tricolour in the highest of regards and achieve bigger and better for her country.

Lately, her knee injury had robbed her of the best, but as they say 'gladiators belong in the Colosseum', she has upped the ante on her with the spate of performances in recent times, her gold medal victory in the Gold Coast 2018, Commonwealth Games being one of them. This incidentally has been characteristic of her entire badminton career and whenever one thought she was down and out, Saina Nehwal has hit back the mantle with vengeance.

Saina's brush with badminton started very early in her life. Her father Dr Harvir Singh and mother Usha Rani, both State-level players, had inclination towards the sport and post their marriage, to keep themselves fit, swung the racquet on a regular basis. Whenever they went to the local court to play badminton they would take little Saina along, introducing her to the sport at a very young age.

In fact in the book *Saina Nehwal: An Inspirational Biography*, renowned journalist T.S. Sudhir has explicitly stated:[2]

> Saina, it would seem, acquired the flair to play badminton from her parents. Both Harvir and Usha are good players and once Chandranshu (Saina's elder sister) became a bit older, the couple picked up the racquet again. It helped that the university residential quarters also housed a badminton court and soon the exploits of Usha and Harvir made them a popular sporting couple.

In fact in the following lines of the same book, T.S. Sudhir also documents that Usha Rani was a better player of the two and in many ways was responsible for Saina picking up the sport as a career option.

A chance opportunity for Dr Harvir Singh to move to Indian Council of Agricultural Research (ICAR) in Hyderabad

---

[2]Sudhir, T.S. 2012. *Saina Nehwal: An Inspirational Biography*. Nimby Books/ Westland.

changed it all for Saina Nehwal. Initially, what started as an effort to involve Saina into something constructive soon turned into a career option and she started moving from strength to strength to prove her metal as a force to reckon with in the world of badminton.

Saina stepped into the world of badminton in May 1999. With the intention of enrolling his daughter in the badminton summer camp organized in Lal Bahadur Shastri Indoor Stadium, one fine day Dr Harvir Singh took Saina to meet coach P.S.S. Nani Prasad. Since there was only a month left for the summer camp to start and all the seats were full, Nani Prasad turned her down.

But Saina's father insisted that Nani Prasad watch his daughter play once and if her game did not excite him, they would leave. On relentless insistence by the enthusiastic father, Nani Prasad agreed to give Saina a chance. She picked up the racquet and the first shot she hit was a smash. The execution instantly impressed the coach and he decided to give her a chance in the summer camp of 1999.

What followed the rest of the summer was a series of events which lead to the rise of a star who went on to win close to twenty-one individual super series titles, a bronze medal in Olympics, achieved the world no. 1 ranking in 2015, and most importantly, made India a force to be reckoned with in the global badminton scene.

Saina's style of playing is very aggressive, which is diametrically opposite to how she is in personal life, and this at times takes her opponent by surprise.

Many can compare Saina's career to a dedicated leader or a CEO of a company who with time has risen in the ranks of the organization, working with an unwavering dedication to make her/his company number one. Like any employee determined to make a mark in the professional world, Saina's initial years were relentless devotion to the art of wielding the badminton racquet first under the tutelage of P.S.S. Nani Prasad then under S.M. Arif, Pullela Gopichand and finally under Vimal Kumar, towards the larger goal of becoming a world-class badminton player.

Those who have seen Saina closely, unanimously agree that it is her dedication which sets her apart from the rest. She like the mighty Arjuna of the Mahabharata is always focused on the eye of the fish and when on the court, nothing can shake her focus. In fact in one of her statements which has now achieved cult status, she openly confesses, 'I want to be the best, it is not about the ranking, it's about being consistent.'[3]

Saina's achievements have been phenomenal and time and again she has been praised by different quarters for her capabilities. Ace shuttler and nine-time national badminton champion, Aparna Popat says:[4]

> Saina's consistency at the top and the titles she has won have helped the game become popular in the country.

---

[3]http://www.azquotes.com/quote/927140

[4]https://www.sportskeeda.com/badminton/amazing-to-see-saina-nehwal-stay-top-for-long-time-aparna-popat

> It's amazing that she was able to stay at the top for so many years. If a player can hang on to the top five of the world rankings for five years, it's incredible. Saina has been doing that and that's a great feat. If you are not consistent, people will just forget you.

Adding to what Aparna Popat says, Prakash Padukone in 2010 said, 'She is the most complete woman shuttler in the world now.'[5] Last but not the least, her coach Pullela Gopichand in 2009 said, 'I think it has been a fantastic performance by Saina in recent years. It has been admirable not just in Indian context but at a global level too.'[6]

After she won the bronze medal in London Olympics, sports personalities from outside the world of badminton also spoke highly of her. Heaping praises, Sachin Tendulkar said:[7]

> Whatever I have seen of her there is no drama involved, it's just quality badminton and that is what you expect from a sportsperson. After winning (bronze medal) also, she has not got carried away and that's the beauty of being a champion sportsperson.

All the praise and adulation do not distract Saina. In fact just like her coach Pullela Gopichand, she is considered to

---

[5]https://www.dawn.com/news/932365

[6]http://indiatoday.intoday.in/story/Gopi+Chand+gives+Indians+a+chance+at+home/1/52923.html

[7]https://www.outlookindia.com/newswire/story/sachin-praises-saina-nehwal-gifts-her-bmw/772573

be very focused and a simple person.

It's not that she did not have her fair share of brush with the world of celebrities, but she found all the glamour and glitter to be detrimental to her performance and goals, and deliberately decided to stay focused on badminton. Case in point, she being considered an expensive celebrity because she barely gives 5–7 days in a year for her brand endorsements, as her calendar is usually crowded with badminton-related commitments.[8]

To excel in any field, one should keep their goals clear and eyes on the future, like Saina always has. For her failures are temporary and do not deter her from focusing on the ultimate glory of being the best in what she does.

She believes it is too early to plan for a future beyond court, but setting up a badminton academy to groom the talent in India and continue contributing to the legacy she started is definitely a part of her plan. Saina has and will always be the poster girl for badminton in India and many will walk on the path taken by her. But what makes her so special and effective? Is it her attitude? Is it her grooming? Is it her never-say-die attitude? Or is it her deft analytical mind?

Through this book we will explore those traits of Saina Nehwal which make her the person she is and how they align to the capabilities of a successful professional, and with which an individual can provide a constructive direction to their career.

---

[8]http://www.afaqs.com/news/story/45433_Saina-Nehwal-Smash-hit-for-brands

It Is a Double's Game: Saina and Her Mentors

> Show me a successful individual and I'll show you someone who had real positive influences in his or her life. I don't care what you do for a living—if you do it well I'm sure there was someone cheering you on or showing the way. A mentor.
>
> —Denzel Washington, Hollywood actor

Saina Nehwal epitomizes the world of badminton in India. She in many ways has been the messiah which badminton fraternity in India was waiting for. But as every messiah has a guiding light showing them the way forward, Saina's mentors have played just as much of an important role in her success.

Many argue on the importance of mentors in one's life.

While some feel it is an over-emphasized concept, there are a few who attribute their rise to a strong mentor. If you open the chapters in the lives of successful sportsmen you will always find a mentor's name associated with them, Sachin Tendulkar—Ramakant Achrekar, Virat Kohli—Raj Kumar Sharma, and Geeta Phogat—Mahavir Phogat to name a few.

But seriously, what can a good mentor do?

To answer this question, from the vaults of Indian history, I would like to pull out the example of a great king and the founder of the Maurya Empire, Chandragupta Maurya and his mentor, Chanakya.

Lead by Chandragupta Maurya, 340–298 BCE saw the rise and expansion of the great Maurya Kingdom. Chandragupta had royal ancestry, but was orphaned and abandoned due to family feud. Raised as their son by a pastoral family, one day while playing with his friends he met the Brahmin strategist and economist, Chanakya.

Humiliated and enraged for his unpleasant appearance by King Dhana Nanda, the ruler of the kingdom of Magadha, Chanakya was returning home when he saw Chandragupta. Impressed by his conduct and approach towards his friends, Chanakya, who had sworn to dethrone Dhana Nanda from his own kingdom, decided to groom Chandragupta to be the next king. Taking permission from Chandragupta's parents, Chanakya took him under his wings and started training him in weapons, warfare, politics and strategy.

As time progressed, Chandragupta grew into a strapping young man who was leading Chanakya's guerilla army of men who had faced atrocities by Dhana Nanda.

Devising a grand plan to invade Pataliputra, a battle was declared against the kingdom's army. The army was drawn from the city to a distant battlefield to engage with Maurya's forces. Maurya's general and spies meanwhile bribed the corrupt generals of Dhana Nanda to disturb the equation with the State's army. Chandragupta and Chanakya also succeeded in creating an atmosphere of civil war in the kingdom, which culminated in the death of the heir to the Magadhan throne. Chanakya through his intelligence and shrewdness managed to win over popular sentiment of Magadha. Out of options, ultimately Dhana Nanda resigned and handed power to Chandragupta Maurya, and went into exile.

In Indian history, you might not find a more concerted effort of dethroning as that of King Dhana Nanda. This piece of history also stands apart because of the equation between Chandragupta Maurya and his mentor, Chanakya, for what Chandragupta Maurya achieved could not have been possible without the guidance of Chanakya. While the actions were of mentee, Chandragupta, the brain behind his every move was of his mentor, Chanakya.

This part of history has always made me wonder about the importance of a mentor. Why is there so much emphasis across disciplines on the importance of mentors? I mean, could a sports personality like Saina have made it big without a mentor?

To understand this better we need to analyse the basic design of a situation or an adversity. Every adversity by design has visible aspects and invisible aspects. While visible aspects are those which one is able to decode by their own past experiences, invisible aspects are like those fine lines on a palm not visible to the naked eye unless observed closely.

Now identification of an issue as visible versus invisible depends upon an individual's experience with those situations in the past. Does this mean that what might be visible to me might be invisible to you and vice versa? Well, the answer is a resounding yes.

Point to be noted over here is your interpretation of a situation depends on what you have experienced in the past. Does this mean you have to undergo each of those situations yourself to learn about it? The answer is no. There is another way to alter or turn the results in your favour or be well-prepared for a situation and that is to talk or seek guidance from those who have more experience than you in that specific field, which is called mentorship in modern world. A mentor does not need to be an expert in the field but could be someone who has more knowledge than you and is able to guide you to steer clear of difficulties.

In Saina's case, she has been fortunate to be mentored by multiple coaches, first of which happened to be in the form of P.S.S. Nani Prasad and her parents, Usha Rani and Dr Harvir Singh.

Had it not been for Dr Harvir Singh's visit to Lal Bahadur Shastri Indoor Stadium in Hyderabad where P.S.S. Nani Prasad saw the talent in Saina, things would have been very different for her.

Post the summer camp of 1999, Prasad's words of encouragement for nine-year-old Saina showed her badminton enthusiastic parents a direction for her career. What followed was a well-planned training program for Saina Nehwal under the guidance and mentorship of Prasad executed to a tee by her parents.

Saina, of course, had a spark and no one can take that away from her, but to spot that and groom the talent into a world-class sportsperson could not have happened without Prasad's initial work. He selectively exposed Saina to the kind of conditions which ensured that she had the hunger to make a mark in the world of badminton.

T.S. Sudhir also wrote in his book that in the summer camp organized in Lal Bahadur Shastri Indoor Stadium, the players were supposed to participate in the elimination matches on the last day of the camp and the winner of the final match was to be selected by Sports Authority of Andhra Pradesh (SAAP) as a regular trainee. In those matches, nine-year-old Saina was wrongly pegged against the much older Anjana Reddy, daughter of Ravi Reddy who is the owner of the Deccan Chronicle group. As expected, young Saina lost to Anjana. Realizing the blunder the authorities had committed, a furious Prasad declared the match null and void and reorganized her match.[1]

In her second chance, Saina lived up to Prasad's expectations of her and went on to be a finalist, where she

---

[1]Sudhir, T.S. 2012. *Saina Nehwal: An Inspirational Biography*. Nimby Books/ Westland.

lost to a girl named Diti. Since Diti was from Nagpur and was only visiting Hyderabad for her summer holidays, she had to leave to go back home and by default the seat went to Saina. Thus began the journey of Saina Nehwal to become the world no. 1 in badminton.[2]

T.S. Sudhir further wrote that Prasad was so sure of Saina's prowess that when he was transferred to Vijayawada, a satellite city in Andhra Pradesh, he had tried to convince Saina's parents to send her to the badminton academy there so that he could continue to coach her, which was declined by her parents for obvious reasons.[3]

What gave Prasad so much of confidence in Saina's abilities? Was it Saina's skills or was it her commitment? I think it was a mix of both.

LEARNING TIP

Mentee-mentor relationship is of equal commitment and hard work. Both need to prove their calibre for a fruitful relationship.

What needs to be understood over here is the way a mentee always wants the best mentor, a mentor too wants to invest himself in a capable mentee. Especially in the corporate world where time is money, no mentor wants to invest his time in

[2]https://www.youtube.com/watch?v=YdUOEE2bQFg

[3]https://www.thenewsminute.com/lives/912

a mentee who might be a lost cause. Great mentors go by reputation, great mentees by their zest to learn.

As far as Saina's success in her initial days is concerned, there was another unsung hero in her life whom people often forget to serenade and who does not come from professional quarters of the Indian badminton system, but from her very own home—Usha Rani.

Saina's mother was a gladiator at heart and in her younger days was known for her exploits with badminton racquets. A self-taught enthusiast she had proved her calibre with the racquet at the State-level. This experience gave Usha Rani a very good understanding of what champions are made of and ensured that Saina was groomed to be the best in her formative years.[4]

Usha Rani was a strict mother and had no qualms in disciplining her children the good old way. When Saina stepped under the tutelage of Prasad, Usha Rani knew that they were boarding for a special journey, to which both she and her husband needed to be committed whole-heartedly. She made sure that Saina got nothing but the best, right from the kitchen to the court.

As a mother she was Saina's biggest critic and support, she analysed her matches and shared her inputs whenever Saina went wrong. Her constant support and constructive criticism helped Saina get a better hold of the game.

One specific incident which still plays loud in Saina's mind

---

[4]http://www.rediff.com/sports/report/my-mother-made-me-think-like-champion-saina/20121203.htm

comes from her initial days when she was an under-10 player. Saina was playing in the semi-final of a tournament that was organized in Thane, Mumbai, where she lost to her opponent. Dejected, as she was returning from the court her mother walked up to her and slapped her. Saina was stunned and silent, but that did not bother Usha Rani because for her losing was not an option and she wanted to make sure that Saina delivers the best always.[5]

Many believe badminton is inexpensive in comparison to other sports, such is not the case. A champion in making has an annual expense of 25–35 lakh, which unless you have a sponsorship is tough for any parent to manage.

Within a couple of years of professional badminton, Saina began frequently travelling abroad to get exposure to the international format and grooming for the sport. This was hard on the Nehwals—they had to make financial commitments beyond their capabilities, but they ensured she never got anything less than the best. All this comes from the belief which the Nehwals had in Saina's abilities. She realizes this too, and at many public forums has acknowledged the many sacrifices that her parents have made for her.

▪

Once Prasad got transferred to Vijayawada and moved out of Saina's life there was a void in guidance that Saina received.

[5]https://timesofindia.indiatimes.com/sports/badminton/I-believe-I-can-become-world-No-1-says-Saina-Nehwal/articleshow/17174646.cms

The Nehwals realized this and quickly moved Saina under the mentorship of S.M. Arif, best known as coach of the likes of Pullela Gopichand and Jwala Gutta. It was a wise decision, which quickly propelled Saina in the badminton world. Saina used to practice along with Arif's male students, which improved her game drastically and within no time she started making impact in tournaments. A junior-level candidate, she soon started participating in senior-level tournaments to get exposure to superior competition and flourish her game.[6]

Saina was not even thirteen when she travelled abroad for the first time, and from there on virtually started living a life out of a suitcase. She regularly travelled with S.M. Arif and his assistant coach, Govardhan Reddy, across the world to participate in various tournaments.[7]

Things under Arif's guidance were different from Prasad's. S.M. Arif had introduced Saina to a larger and fast-evolving international environment and a belief that she could compete in it. He also focused extensively on core muscles of Saina's body to make her a much stronger player.

Arif knew Saina was a star in the making even before she came under his fold. Seeing her practicing in the Lal Bahadur Shastri Indoor Stadium, he had predicted that she will be India's reply to China's dominance in world badminton.

As per Arif, Saina was a strongly built girl and would never say no to practice or a new regime. Realizing that

---

[6]https://www.thenewsminute.com/lives/912

[7]Ibid.

she was way better than her opponents in the junior circuit, he introduced Saina to the senior circuit and she justified her coach's confidence in her by quickly making a mark in that circuit and won her first junior international title of Czechoslovakia Junior Open in 2003.[8]

While it is tough to achieve such vertical rise in the court of professional world, there are a few individuals who have had aggressive growth path compared to others with similar experience. One such example could be of Google's CEO, Sundar Pichai, who has been mentored by Larry Page himself. The right-hand man of Page, Sundar, time and again through his diligence and hard work, has proved himself worthy of the support he enjoys from him, leading him to grow to the ranks of the organization's CEO within a short span of twelve years.

LEARNING TIP

Have measurement criteria to measure success of a mentorship programme.

One learning factor from both the above examples is that frequency of positive outcomes from mentorship should form an important criterion of measurement, as a constant dialogue with below par results is effort wasted for both the mentor and mentee. It is somewhat like a sailor relying on a

[8]https://www.thenewsminute.com/lives/912

faulty compass which though might point north but a degree or two of variation might get interpreted into miles offset from the original destination. A good mentor and mentee relationship ensures positive outcomes often.

▪

In 2004, Saina moved under the guidance of Pullela Gopichand. Saina by then was already a force to be reckoned with in the domestic circuit, she was known for her aggressive style of playing which also happened to be Gopichand's brand of game as well. What Gopichand did was expose Saina to a wider range of shot selection and a mental conditioning necessary to be a champion on the global platform. It was more of a fine-tuning process for Saina.

There are quite a few takeaways for anyone who observes Saina and her relationships with her mentors.

First and foremost is the level of confidence vested by them in each other. Although Saina has been coached by four different coaches, one thing which all of them agree upon unanimously is the blind faith she has in her coaches. She is known to dedicate herself whole-heartedly to their training and implements their vision in the court.

LEARNING TIP

A professional should first try to be a diligent student to his/her art and then to his/her mentors.

One thing which any professional can learn from this is to be a diligent student to your art first and then to your mentors. Majority of professionals commit the mistake of coming to the professional world with preconceived notions and a 'know-it-all' attitude. While the professional schools teach you the disciplines, they do not arm you with the necessary survival skills to succeed in the professional world. One of the most important things which everyone should do as soon as they step into the professional world is identify a supportive mentor within the organization and seek regular guidance from them. Diligence and constructive conversation should be the base of this relationship with the ultimate goal of becoming more effective in the professional environment.

LEARNING TIP

Having a mentor is not being ineffective but an effort to be more effective.

A real life example I have in front of me which emphasizes the importance of a mentor would be of one of my friends, Arjun Dixit. When Arjun started his career he believed that he knew it all and never worked towards identifying a mentor. He did not even believe in socializing with his seniors, the result was a stunted growth with a limited understanding of conducting himself professionally. Six to seven years later, sometime in the middle of his career, we had an open conversation about the importance and benefits of mentoring, where I convinced him to try mentorship as an experiment. Taking my suggestion half-heartedly, he approached a couple of seniors in his organization who were known for their mentorship, fortunately for him one of them agreed to guide him, and in a matter of 2–3 years he had a phenomenal turnaround from a nobody to a somebody. Now working as a director in a reputed organization, he himself is a strong advocate of mentorship program and has made it one of the pillars of his department culture.

LEARNING TIP

The more vertical the climb, the more support you need. A mentor is most helpful in such a situation.

If you observe closely, you would realize that Saina, besides being talented, was also an exceptional student of the sport, never letting her massive success hinder her learning path. In many ways, she was a destiny's child, born to become a success story in the world of badminton—but that never let her become overconfident, on the contrary she always stayed hungry to grow and hone her skills.

Majority of people as they move up the ladder become prey to their success and very often forget that the traits and skill which brought them to that point will not be enough to take them forward. It is important to constantly keep learning and be surrounded with those who provide you sound guidance. Success should never stop you from learning, on the contrary it is more important for a successful person to learn more and faster in order to be incrementally effective. In management discipline, there is a borrowed concept from the evolutionary hypothesis called the 'Red Queen Effect'. Coined by Leigh Van Valen, the hypothesis suggests, 'To be at the same place one has to run faster continuously.' The phenomenon's name is derived from a statement that the Red Queen made to Alice in Lewis Carroll's *Through the Looking-Glass, and What Alice Found There* (a sequel to *Alice's Adventures in Wonderland*), in her explanation of the nature of the Looking-Glass Land she said: 'Now, here, you see, it takes all the running you can do, to keep in the same place.'

Van Valen coined the hypothesis's name as Red Queen Effect because under this interpretation, species have to 'run' or evolve in order to stay in the same place, or else they go extinct.

Moving up the success ladder is a lot like that and there is only one way to make sure that you stay ahead—by being a diligent student to the art and science of the skill you wield rather than be consumed by complacency and a relaxed attitude.

▪

Mentor–Mentee Relationship

A true mentor–mentee relationship goes a long way, probably way beyond day-to-day guidance to envisioning one's shortcomings and preparing them for adversities. Case in point would be Saina's days with S.M. Arif, once Saina started travelling the international circuit, he categorically instructed his assistant coach, Govardhan Reddy, to keep Saina away from the senior players as they already had a negative mindset where they saw themselves as inferior to foreign players and this might affect Saina's thought process. Had this not been done, Saina might not have been as aggressive and as successful a player as she is today.[9]

In Saina's case, things quickly moved northbound once she was under the tutelage of Pullela Gopichand. While she was already a hot name on the anvil of Indian badminton, Gopichand provided her an international perspective. Saina has been very open and upfront about Gopichand's contribution to what she is now. In true 'Guru–Shishya' tradition, she has literally allowed him to steer her around the corridors of international badminton, which Gopichand has honoured by making her a successful badminton player.

Those who have observed Gopichand's influence on Saina are at times surprised at the level of control he exercises. But for Saina, this is her unwavering faith in Gopichand and may be that is the reason, whenever she has stepped out to train under another coach, she has always returned back under his wings.

Many see a reflection of Gopichand in the way Saina conducts herself and it does not surprise me, because while

---

[9]https://www.dailyo.in/sports/saina-nehwal-world-number-1-badminton-first-indian-woman/story/1/2834.html

Saina was still grasping the basics of badminton, Gopichand was busy replicating success of Prakash Padukone by winning the coveted All England Open. In badminton fraternity he was considered a demigod then, but a career cut short due to injury directed him to take up the next best thing he enjoyed—coaching young talent.

As Gopichand launched his badminton academy in Hyderabad, he started attracting the best young talent from all over the country. One thing lead to another and all of a sudden an impressionable Saina was standing in front of her role model gearing up to be trained by him and many are privy that she picked up the tricks of the trade to the tee.

Such was the level of sincerity Saina had towards Gopichand that she followed his instructions like sermons. T.S. Sudhir explained one such instance when Saina lost in the quarterfinals of 2008 Beijing Olympics. She was very dejected and all efforts made by Gopichand to uplift her mood were failing. Out of options, Gopichand jokingly told Saina to report for practice at 6.00 a.m. the following morning. Such were Gopichand's words for Saina that she nodded her head at the instruction and asked in all sincerity if they could instead start at 7.00 a.m.[10]

To find a mentor–mentee equation like Saina and Pullela Gopichand's in professional world might be tough. But an example that comes close is of Don Graham ex-CEO of *The Washington Post* and Sheryl Sandberg COO of Facebook.

---

[10]Sudhir, T.S. 2012. *Saina Nehwal: An Inspirational Biography*. Nimby Books/ Westland.

In 2005, when Mark Zuckerberg was shadowing Don Graham to learn how CEOs are supposed to conduct themselves, Don suggested he recruit his mentee Sheryl Sandberg, and also had a word with Sheryl to accept Mark's offer even though Zuckerberg was younger to her.[11] Sheryl was at the time working for Google as Vice President for its Online Sales division.

LEARNING TIP

Involve your mentor in your major decisions, because a sound advice goes a long way.

Google then being a way bigger name then Facebook, many considered Sheryl's move suicidal. But she trusted her mentor Don's advice. Don played the role of a facilitator between Sheryl and Mark, and the rest is history. It is well-known today how important Sheryl is now in the larger picture of Facebook as a company.

In Anthony K. Tjan's article 'What the Best Mentors do',[12] he talks about common traits of successful mentors. According to him the one factor that is common among all successful mentors is that they try to imprint their 'goodness' on to others in ways that make others feel like fuller versions

[11]https: / / www.inc.com / ilan-mochari / visit-india-creativity.html

[12]'What the Best Mentors Do'.Tjan, Anthony K. 27 February 2017. *Harvard Business Review*.

of themselves.

In other words, the best leaders practice a form of leadership that is less about creating followers and more about creating other leaders, and how do they do it?

1. **Relationship over mentorship**. For the true mentorship to succeed, there needs to exist a chemistry between a mentor and a mentee. As per Anthony's study, genuine intercollegial relationships between mentor and mentee go greater distance than any well-planned mentorship program.
2. **Focus on character and not on competency**. According to Anthony, the best leaders go beyond mentoring necessary competencies for a given position, and focus on helping to shape other people's characters, values, self-awareness, empathy and capacity for respect. They know that in the long run, value-based qualities matter more than skill enhancement. There are many ways to mentor people around these values and to build greater self-awareness.
3. **Let your optimism rule over your cynicism**. Mentees often come up with some puerile ideas or unrealistic ambitions. Try considering all prospects of an idea, before you think of refuting it. Anthony proposes an approach called the '24×3 rule for optimism', where he suggests each time you hear a new idea, see if it is possible for you to spend 24 seconds, 24 minutes, or a day thinking about all the reasons that the idea is good before you criticize any aspect of it.

4. **Place the relationship with your mentee above the company**. The best mentors give more importance to leadership as a duty and service toward others, and inspire commitment by being fully and selflessly committed to the best interests of their colleagues and employees. The aim is not only to unearth a mentee's strengths, but also to understand his/her true passion and to help them find their calling.

He concludes by saying, 'the best mentors avoid overriding the dreams of their mentees. If an employee and a job aren't a good fit, or if an ambitious employee realistically has limited upward growth in a company, a good mentor can help that employee move on. They might be better suited to another role within the organization, or even to a new path somewhere else.

At its highest level, mentorship is about being 'good people' and having the right sort of good people around us—individuals committed to helping others become fuller versions of who they are.

One classic example from the corporate world which justifies the 'Being Good People' thought would be of Richard Branson and his mentor, Sir Freddie Laker. When Branson was establishing the Virgin Atlantic airline, he often ran into trouble and needed direction on the way forward. That's when legendary airline entrepreneur Sir Freddie Laker, a man he had always admired, stepped in. He became a source of help and inspiration during the initial days of Virgin Atlantic. Laker capitalized on his own experience in the airline industry and gave Branson sound advice on how to establish a successful business.

Branson has admitted, 'We wouldn't have gotten anywhere in the airline industry without Freddie's down-to-earth wisdom. He helped shape our vision for high quality service at competitive prices, and was the first to bring to my attention how fiercely we would have to battle with other airlines to make a success of our airline.'

LEARNING TIP

Always show respect to your guides, a lot of you could not have been possible without them.

While Virgin Atlantic airline was preparing to hit the tarmac, they ran into the problem of identifying the right marketing strategy since they did not have as deep pockets as their competitors. In pitched Sir Freedie Laker again and advised Richard Branson to become the face of the company and use his public image to provide the necessary fire power to the launch.

Recalling his advice Branson said, '"Use yourself. Make a fool of yourself. Otherwise you won't survive." That piece of advice influenced my entire approach to business,' he says. 'I took his advice on board and have been thinking up fun ways to stand out from the crowd ever since. I've found by standing out in fun and different ways, your chances of ending up on the front page of the newspaper, rather than the back, are much higher.'[13]

To say the least, a relationship of a mentor and mentee if nothing else is of faith. Selflessness is required to define this relationship, the more selfless the mentor is the stronger the bond is as in the case of Saina and Gopichand.

In 2014, once Gopichand took on the responsibility of being the national coach he was left with less time for Saina, to add to it the likes of Sindhu and K. Srikanth started demanding his attention as well. Recuperating from injuries and making her way back to the centre stage after a break, Saina needed undivided attention. Purely for professional reasons, she decided to change her coach and started training with Vimal Kumar in Bengaluru.

Incidentally, Kumar was one of the few who in 2006 after Saina's win in the Philippines Open under the guidance of Pullela Gopichand had prophesied the rise of Saina Nehwal to the top spot in the world of badminton. In his own words, 'She has tremendous self-belief. She wasn't satisfied with just beating the world no. 4, but went for the title. Most other players win a few good matches but never the title. If she keeps up the momentum, Saina can break into the world's top ten sooner than anyone expects.'[14]

---

[13]https: / / www.forbes.com / sites / alisoncoleman / 2016 / 04 / 10 / why-mentors-can-be-the-making-of-entrepreneurs-like-branson / #57cffa0c1778

[14]https: / / www.dailyo.in / sports / saina-nehwal-world-number-1-badminton-first-indian-woman / story / 1 / 2834.html

LEARNING TIP

It takes a village to get mentored, hold on to your past mentors and work with new ones whenever opportunity shows up.

While under the guidance of Vimal Kumar, Saina identified aspects of her game which she had not explored under Gopichand's coaching. Vimal Kumar concentrated on bleeding confidence of Saina first, building her up morally and technically, he improved certain facets of her game which helped Saina regain lost confidence and position and become the world no. 1 badminton player in the year 2015. After working with Vimal Kumar for three years Saina decided to move back to Pullela Gopichand and Sports Authority of India (SAI) newly appointed Malaysian coach Mulyo Handoyo. Announcing it on Twitter, she wrote: 'Hi friends I wanted to share some news with everyone. For a while I've been thinking about moving my training base back to the Gopichand Academy and I had a discussion about this with Gopi Sir and I am really thankful to him for agreeing to help me again. At this stage in my career, I think he can help me achieve my goals.'

Vimal Kumar was satisfied with Saina's decision and saw it as a move in the best interest of her game and country, and will benefit Saina in the long run and that in principle defines a true mentor.

■

Multiple Mentorship

Off late, like evolution of any other concept, mentorship has undergone its fair share of makeovers and a recent model which has been knocking the doors of management quarters is the concept of 'Multiple Mentorship' which suggests having many mentors instead of one.

The concept of Multiple Mentorship is somewhat comparable to subject specialists in an institution or a school. While one single teacher cannot have expertise in all subjects, hence, a school has teachers teaching multiple disciplines, similarly the idea behind Multiple Mentorship is to gain guidance from many mentors instead of one at a given point.

There is a growing bevy of people in the management world who advocate the benefits of multiple mentors. Probably its only downside being that one might get confused with too much advice, in which case it is best to follow the rule of majority.

While Saina never had multiple coaches/mentors at one given point of time, from a time scale perspective, she has benefited from being coached by multiple mentors who in many ways have enhanced her style of playing. So, while P.S.S. Nani Prasad gave her the necessary grooming in the initial years of her career, S.M. Arif gave her the right exposure and mental conditioning, along with an aggressive style of playing. Pullela Gopichand brought his international experience into play and widened her mental conditioning by developing her badminton skills to international standards, and Vimal Kumar built her confidence and made certain course corrections to ensure putting her back on track.

In corporate life, where jobs are changed often, the concept of Multiple Mentorship makes more sense for the executives. Each company has its own style of working and in such scenarios it becomes important that you have a mentor within the organization to guide you, while holding onto your mentors from previous organizations and tapping into their rich experience. What Multiple Mentorship also does is it acts as the sounding board of one mentor's suggestion with another, helping you in the process to make a well-thought-out, comprehensive decision.

In fact one of my friends who is a CMO with a renowned UK-based multinational company often attributes his professional rise at the age of just thirty-seven to the multiple mentors he had in his life. His mantra is: 'You should have at least five mentors on your speed dial, else you are doing something wrong.' He confesses that there have been times when he did not have a clue on how to deal with situations, but thanks to his network of experienced mentors he has always been able to find answers.

Chanakya too had beautifully summarized this in his book, *Chanakya Neeti*. He wrote, 'Learn from the mistakes of others, you can't live long enough to make them all yourselves.'

Saina has matured over time: from a teenaged badminton sensation to an unstoppable winning force—from world no. 1 to fighting her way back into form, she has seen it all and every time she walked on that path there was always someone walking close behind her ensuring that she was in the right direction—a mentor.

She is well-aware of being an icon whom a generation of badminton players look up to and justifies it by interacting with youngsters, motivating them about how to give their best and sharing her experiences with them the way her mentors did.

Someday she intends to pass on what she has learnt over the years by opening a badminton academy in Haryana, her home State. While the academy is just a thought at this point of time, her desire to contribute to the rising interest in the Indian badminton scene is quite evident.

Being the Best: The Saina Nehwal Way

> We have this culture valued at Uber, which we call the champions' mindset. And champions' mindset isn't always about winning. It's about putting everything you have on the field, every ounce of passion and energy you have. And if you get knocked down, overcoming adversity.
>
> —Travis Cordell Kalanick, co-founder, Uber

Perseverance

I was talking to a renowned gym instructor from Hyderabad about the ideal amount of time that should be spent on strengthening exercises—he told me anything more than a couple of hours a day is more than enough. Bringing variables into discussion I asked him what it would be for a nine-year-old girl. The instructor stared at me and asked with an animated face, 'Why would a nine-year-old go to gym?'

A nine-year-old Saina sure did. In fact, she used to spend two to three hours every day focusing on her strength and stamina. For many, this might be mindless subjecting to unnecessary torture, but not for the Nehwals. Saina was just priming herself up for cutting down the time variable of the growth curve for an early start in her life.

This approach is applicable in any other kind of professional life as well. In an Indian context, usually an aspirant who desires to step into the professional world identifies their skills/interests/specialization only when confronted with the daunting question of the profession they want to get into. To add to it they are often found confused and shuffling between too many options in order to have another career to fall back on. Call it pressure from families or fear of unpredictability we usually do not do a good job when it comes to pursuing our dreams.

A general observation is that those who are well exposed to the nuances of the profession of their choice and have been accustomed to discussing their interests freely in the social circles, tend to have a lot more clarity about what they want to do and are relatively more successful when they join the profession of their interest.

The badminton court has always been Saina's second home; as a child every day she would travel down to Lal Bahadur Shastri Indoor Stadium for her practice. During her schooldays she practiced five hours daily, divided into morning and evening sessions, which used to go up to ten hours during offs and vacations. The time spent on the court was nothing less than austerity, where with unwavering dedication she focused on learning the art of wielding the racquet.

At this point it would be wise to bring in a debate widely known and marketed as the '10,000-Hour Rule' of deliberate practice coined by Malcom Gladwell in his book, *Outliers: The Story of Success*, which goes as:[15]

> The 10,000-hours rule says that if you look at any kind of cognitively complex field, from playing chess to being a neurosurgeon, we see this incredibly consistent pattern that you cannot be good at that unless you practice for 10,000 hours, which is roughly ten years, if you think about four hours a day.

However there were several who challenged the universal applicability of this rule, which brought Malcom Gladwell to defend himself in one of the statements made by him on Reddit.com, where he categorically said:

> There is a lot of confusion about the 10,000 rule that I talk about in *Outliers*. It doesn't apply to sports. And practice isn't a SUFFICIENT condition for success. I could play chess for [a] 100 years and I'll never be a

[15]Gladwell, Malcolm. 2008. *Outliers: The Story of Success*. Little, Brown and Company.

grandmaster. The point is simply that natural ability requires a huge investment of time in order to be made manifest. Unfortunately, sometimes complex ideas get oversimplified in translation.

However, there is a parallel thought coined by Cal Newport in his book *So Good They Can't Ignore You*, which does not exactly endorse Malcom Gladwell's rule applicability in sports, but delves on how you practice is important. According to it, what makes ridiculously successful people so successful is they are experts at practicing—they can push themselves to the exact limit of their skillset and thus expand their abilities day after day. If you're not expanding yourself in such a fashion—you'll never be ridiculously successful.[16]

LEARNING TIP

Nothing can substitute perseverance. No one is born with a skill, it is something which you learn over time.

This, in other words, means 'outliers' or people who go beyond the realm of normal to establish themselves as winners.

If we try to summarize the discussion above, one would understand the key to mastery of any skill is in the

[16]http://www.businessinsider.in/Malcolm-Gladwell-Explains-What-Everyone-Gets-Wrong-About-His-Famous-10000-Hour-Rule/articleshow/35964144.cms

practice and desire to master it. Merely spending 4–5 hours daily without the intention of improving oneself is not the suggestion of either Malcom Gladwell or Cal Newport. After all, there is a reason it said that, 'God is in the details.'

Will to Win

A story on willpower which always catches my fancy every time I come across it is of the Brooklyn Bridge.

In 1870, a visionary and dedicated engineer named John Roebling was motivated by an idea to build a bridge connecting New York to Long Island. However, bridge engineers and experts across the world thought that it was an impossible feat and discouraged him.

But John Roebling could not ignore his dream. He envisioned and thought about it all the time, and knew deep in his heart that it was possible. After discussing his idea with many, he managed to convince his son Washington Roebling, an engineer too, that the bridge in fact could be built.

Working together the father and son developed concepts of how the objective could be achieved and how the hurdles could be resolved. Confident about their skills and grasp over the subject, the inspired and motivated father–son duo recruited a crew and began constructing the bridge.

In just a few months of the construction project being underway, a tragic accident on the site killed John Roebling. Son Washington was injured as well with partial brain damage, leaving him paralysed.

Although surrounded by criticism from all sides, Washington Roebling never lost his will to complete the bridge in spite of his paralysis.

As he lay on his hospital bed with the sunlight streaming through the windows, a gentle breeze blew the curtains apart and he was able to see the sky and the trees outside. He felt it was a sign. Suddenly an idea struck him. All he could do was move one finger and with it he developed a code of communication with his wife.

He touched his wife's arm with the movable finger, indicating that he wanted her to call the engineers again. Using the same technique, he instructed the engineers little by little on what to do and soon the project was back on track.

For thirteen years from his apartment with a view of the progress, Washington tapped out his instructions with his finger on his wife's arm till the bridge was completed.

Today, even after 134 years of its construction, the outstanding Brooklyn Bridge stands gloriously, as a tribute to the victory of one man's indomitable spirit, his knowledge and skill of bridge construction and his willpower to not be defeated by the circumstances.

Personally, I find this a fantastic story of a man's unwavering confidence in his skills which led him to develop a will to an obsessive level, and as a result we now stare at one of the biggest marvels of human history.

■

Saina used to live about 25 kms away from Lal Bahadur Shastri Indoor Stadium in a locality called Rajendra Nagar. For a practice which would start at 6.00 a.m., she would wake up at 4.00 a.m. While her father accompanied her to the morning sessions, it was her mother who accompanied her for the evening practice. These sessions would start with strenuous warm-up exercises, followed by hours of practice on the court. But she never gave up on the hard routine and was always ready for a challenge.

So, what exactly makes her the player she is? Is it her will? Or is it her skill?

Just like the Roebling father–son duo, it is her willpower, skill and grasp over the subject which makes her a winner.

Talk to her coaches and you will hear one common feedback, 'Saina is a very hard-working girl who likes to win in whatever she does.'

Those who have seen her at close quarters know that she is driven by a very strong desire to win. Anything to do with badminton is a competition for Saina, which she does not like to lose. Even for an activity as trivial as warm-up sprints, she puts in her best and this is the attitude which defines her success.

Early in her career she did not have an amazing range of shots to offer, however, what compensated for range was her burning will to win. Providing some fodder to ponder further on this is S.M. Arif, who in one of his observations insights that Saina was very competitive and liked to excel in the smallest of the things on the court. Her will to win would compensate for the aspects she was not particularly strong in.

Aparna Popat in one of her blogs had said:[17]

> I first played Saina at the Senior Nationals in 2004, when she was fourteen years old. While I realized that what Gopi said about her strength was true, what really stood out for me was her never-say-die approach that was evident even then. She really toiled through the match never giving up on hope even though I was the top-seed and by then national champion six times over.

■

Whenever asked about her mental conditioning, she always attributes it to her mother, Usha Rani. A former sportswoman herself, her mother always pushed Saina to do her best and planted the Olympic dream in her mind at a very young age. She always told her, 'Saina you have to get an Olympic medal for me,' to which Saina just smiled till it actually happened.[18]

In the years leading up to the 2012 Olympics in London where Saina won the bronze medal, she was not particularly at the top of her game, 2010 and 2011 saw her struggling with her form. Many questioned on whether Saina had already

---

[17]http://www.firstpost.com/blogs/how-saina-overcame-her-shortcomings-to-win-an-olympic-medal-407117.html

[18]'Walk The Talk' with Badminton Champion Saina Nehwal. NDTV. 9 January 2015. https://www.youtube.com/watch?v=VnA5LRnwzVA

peaked, but she proved all her critics and detractors wrong, with concerted efforts on improving her ligament injury and regimented practice sessions in a short frame of time she bounced back in the international badminton scene. It looked as if she had a point to prove.

Aparna Popat gives insight on Siana's Olympic win:[19]

> I have seldom come across someone so committed in any field of life. So persevering to prove themselves, so determined to win. Her unfortunate loss in the quarterfinals of the Beijing Games spurred her on to prepare 100 percent for London 2012. Today, I feel immensely happy and proud that Saina has achieved her dream of an Olympic medal because I don't think I can think of anyone who deserves it more.

Another story of courage and determination in sports which resonates with Saina's struggle during the months before the London Olympics and has always inspired me too is of the former Austrian Formula One driver, Niki Lauda.

A lanky Niki was always a racer at heart, joining Ferrari in 1974 he won the Formula One title for them in 1975. However, by 1975 Niki Lauda was also at loggerheads with James Hunt, the flashy British driver who was known for his wild antics off the racing track as much as on it. Hunt had won the race at the Dutch Grand Prix that year, but Lauda had won the championship.

---

[19]http: / /www.firstpost.com/blogs/how-saina-overcame-her-shortcomings-to-win-an-olympic-medal-407117.html

Dutch Grand Prix led to the beginning of a career-long bittersweet relationship between the two drivers. Soon both the racers got consumed by mindless competition which grew stronger over the years, but a key race in 1976 turned out to be different for them.

Consumed by obsession to one up on James Hunt, during the German Grand Prix, Lauda lost control of his car and crashed it, immediately bursting into flames. His bones broken, Lauda could not escape quickly and he damaged his lungs and received burns on his head and wrists. He later slipped into a coma, hinting at a possible retirement once he recovered. But the accident did something unbelievable to Lauda, he recovered from the coma with an iron-like determination and focus to get back on track. In six weeks he was back on his feet and ready to comeback. However, he could not perform to his potential in the Japanese Grand Prix and bailed out of the race after a few laps.

He came back stronger in the year 1977 and with his iron will and dedication won the F1 championship that year. Niki Lauda's focus and persistence had paid off.

LEARNING TIP

Failure is a myth for achievers. They only see it as either victory or learning experiences.

For achievers the concept of a ringside view does not exist, either you are in the game or you're not; knocked out or the winner.

Another person known for his persistence and never-say-die attitude was Steve Jobs. He did not always have things easy for him. Right from the days when he faced cut-throat competition from Microsoft, to being asked by his own company's board of directors to leave Apple Computers, to setting up another company called NeXT Computer, which was eventually acquired by Apple leading him to subsequently becoming the CEO of the company, he had seen it all—the good, the bad and the best.

Even when he formed and lead NeXT Computer, he always envisioned going back to Apple and changing things. Imagine how it all would have spanned out if he had given up on his vision midway and taken an easier path? Apple would probably not have been the brand it is now and mankind would have been a couple of notches below where the global technology stands at this point in time.

Imagine a situation where a company which had shown you the door is now reaching out to you and rolling out a red carpet for you? Nothing can give you a high bigger than that. Steve Jobs in many ways is a classic example of what a person can achieve in professional life if he/she sets their mind to something.

Saina is an athlete extraordinare. Just like Steve Jobs, she has slipped in her career many a times only to emerge stronger each time and set benchmarks only few can imagine.

In business management, there is a coaching model called Skill vs Will Matrix made popular by Max Landsberg. It is used to measure the motivation levels of people and to what extent can they be relied upon to deliver results.[20]

Skill		Will: Low	Will: High
	High	Low attention span, skilled professional. **High–Low**	Skilled professional looking to excel. **High–High**
	Low	Nervous unskilled professional. **Low–Low**	Enthusiastic and unskilled professional. **Low–High**

Figure 1

In Figure 1, there are four quadrants under which any person's skill and will levels can be measured.

1. Low Skill–Low Will: Regulate and motivate

Low skills and low will is a difficult combination to manage. The coach or manager's role in such cases is very important and requires both taking charge and inspiring the concerned person. Management in such cases needs to get in solid rules, control and decision-making. Such kind of a person is usually

[20]https://danspira.com/2010/04/11/skill-will-matrix-revisited-taking-the-employee%E2%80%99s-point-of-view/

negative, requires a lot of efforts to be brought back on track and should ideally be considered on fence as far as the future is concerned.

2. High Skill–Low Will: Train the person

Coaching in such scenarios is mostly a motivational role. Such people have the necessary skills to execute the job. All that a manager needs to do is to inculcate confidence and enthusiasm in the worker. Decision-making continues to be the coach or manager's responsibility, but communication between the two parties will be the key. The coach/manager should aspire to have the employee take charge of his responsibilities eventually.

3. Low Skill–High Will: Nurturing the person

This situation usually arises with new talent who are eager to perform, get off to a flyer and make a good impression. The coaching style for such people is usually aimed at controlling and guiding the concerned person's actions and supporting them in their decisions.

4. High Skill–High Will: Delegation to the person

These are the easiest kind of people to manage. The coach/manager in such scenarios need to give a lot of freedom and responsibilities to the employee and get involved only when necessary. These human resources are the future stars of the organization and for the exact same reason, the coach/manager should keep a close eye on the progress of the resource, in order to set challenging goals and ensure a high level of motivation constantly.

The first question one usually asks when introduced to the above concept is that what the ideal zone/range is. Well, it depends from profession to profession—but both the quadrants on the right are the suggested space for anyone who wants to make a dent in their field. If one shows will and plenty of skill, then it does not take long before they can become a juggernaut in their profession.

While will is an internal factor—an outcome of a person's desire to succeed, skill is something one acquires over time by being introduced to concepts or situations relevant to one's profession. The success of an individual, however, depends on how well-prepared he is for the big stage, and that is where you need superior mentoring.

So while a plethora of skills is like an arrow without a bow, burning will is like a bow without an arrow. Both are needed in right measure and trajectory to hit the bullseye.

In Saina's case, if we try to map her during different stages of her life it becomes evident that she has always been a wonderful student to her sport. If we go by what her mentors have to say, she has always been very competitive, which is the outcome of a strong will. Hence, you will see her at the extreme right of the matrix throughout, representing a high level of will, more so hovering towards the top right quadrant.

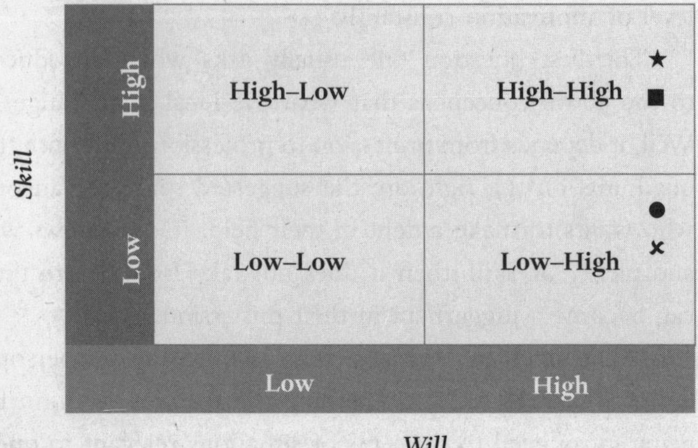

Figure 2

Figure 2 indicates that Saina began her career with relatively low skill but a tremendous amount of will as represented by the cross icon in the figure. This would be the time frame when she was between 9–11 years old.

LEARNING TIP

Skill and will both go hand in hand. Lack of either is not an option for champions.

Two years later, she continued to show a tremendous amount of will while aggressively progressing on the skill parameter as represented by the circle icon in the figure. This would be her age bracket of 12–14 years.

Once she moved under coach Pullela Gopichand in 2014, things started progressing rapidly on the skill parameter—evolving her into a champion and a ranked player in the world of badminton, as represented by first the square and ultimately by the star icon in the figure. This would be say from 2004, the age bracket of 15–22 years.

For all professionals the concept of skill and will is very important. Young professionals often join an organization with high expectations, which is a wrong approach. In the initial years, one should focus only on learning and honing their skills; and contribute to the set-up only after they're confident. A point that should be noted here is that while this learning curve could be steep for some, it usually takes around 5–6 years for one to master a professional skill.

Discipline

In Sanskrit, we have very profound words dedicated to discipline:

> *Vidya dadati vinayam, vinayam dadati patratam |*
> *Patratvaddhanamapnoti, dhanaddharmam tatah sukham ||*
>
> True knowledge gives discipline, from discipline comes worthiness, from worthiness one gets wealth, from wealth one does good deeds and from that comes joy.

Sports personalities in every way epitomize the value of discipline in one's life. Day in, day out without losing the sight of their aim, they relentlessly practice their sports till they become the beacon of what they represent.

Saina, as mentioned before, travelled 25 kilometres one way twice a day to practice atleast six hours every day relentlessly for ten long years. It takes an exceptional amount of determination and discipline to repeat the same routine every day, and more so after you achieve the dizzying heights of success.

Since 2009, Saina has been among the top badminton players in the world and even ranked the world no. 1 in the year 2015. It takes years of discipline to reach and maintain oneself in such a league. Even now, whenever someone calls in for a practice session Saina is usually the first to report on the court with her gear.

Anil Kumble's success story in cricket is also very similar to Saina's. Kumble was neither a child prodigy like Sachin Tendulkar, nor gifted like Muttiah Muralitharan. The three pillars on which he captured the imagination of the entire cricketing fraternity were—dedication, discipline and resolve. Over time, he mastered the art of balling and strategizing against the opposition player. Quieter one of the lot, in the dressing room his energy was always focused on contributing the maximum to the team's performance.

If you look at the routines of professionals with exceptional success in their fields, you would realize there is a fair amount of discipline in the way they conduct themselves. Morning to evening, doing the same routine gives them a sense of discipline and ability to focus on the larger goals ahead of them.

LEARNING TIP

Life is all about pains, either you take pain of discipline and succeed or you take the pain of failure and repent

Summarizing the thoughts above, entreprenuer, author and motivational speaker, Jim Rohn once said:

> 'Success in nothing more than a few simple disciplines practiced every day.'

Those who have observed the way Saina has conducted herself in the last eighteen years of her life would agree with it.

But what does this mean in the professional world? The one thing which comes out clearly is that discipline is the bridge between a person's aspirations and his goal. He or she cannot anticipate success by taking shortcuts. Relentless pursuit of one's dream with absolute discipline is the only fuel which willpower you to the top of your game.

Remember, in a crowd there are always two kinds of people—those who clap and those who are being clapped for. What differentiates between the two kinds is hard work, sincerity, vision, confidence and an underlying desire to be the best in the field.

Saina could not have become 'Champion Saina' without working hard on the strategy prepared by her coaches and following her own vision to excel in the game. It takes sweat, blood and sacrifices to go from being the brat of the house to becoming the poster girl for badminton and then graduating to being a badminton legend who inspires a whole generation.

Attitude Par Excellence

> Ability is what you're capable of doing. Motivation determines what you do. Attitude determines how well you do it.
>
> —Lou Holtz, former American football player

Have you heard of the Battle of Saragarhi where twenty-one Sikh soldiers of the British Indian Army fought against 10,000 Pashtun warriors?

Not many know about this gritty story of gallantry where the attitude of these Sikh soldiers from 36th Sikhs (now known as 4th Battalion of the Sikh Regiment) turned out to be mightier than the strength of 10,000 Afghan soldiers. This story has of late caught a lot of attention and there has been a book, a TV show and a film made on the same.

To briefly tell you the story, Saragarhi was a small village in the border district of Kohat, situated on the Samana Range, in present-day Pakistan. From a regiment of Sikh Soldiers created on 20 April 1894, five companies of the 36th Sikhs under the command of Lt. Col. John Haughton, were sent to the North West Frontier Province (Khyber-Pakhtunkhwa) in August 1897, and were stationed at Samana Hills, Kurag, Sangar, Sahtop Dhar and Saragarhi.

The British had partially succeeded in getting control of this volatile area, however, the tribal Pashtuns attacked British personnel from time to time. Thus, a series of forts originally built by Maharaja Ranjit Singh, ruler of the Sikh Empire, were consolidated. Two of the forts were Fort Lockhart on the Hindu Kush Mountains and Fort Gulistan on the Sulaiman Range situated a few miles apart. As the two forts were not visible to each other, Saragarhi was created midway, as a lighthouse communication post. The Saragarhi post was situated on a rocky elevation and consisted of a small block house with fortifications and a signalling tower.

A rebellion by the Afghans began there in 1897, and between 27 August and 11 September that year several surge attacks by Pashtuns to capture the forts were neutralized by the regiment. On 9 September 1897, Afridi tribes, in allegiance with the Afghans, attacked Fort Gulistan. Both the attacks were neutralized and reinforcement from Fort Lockhart, on its return trip, reinforced the signalling detachment positioned at Saragarhi, increasing its strength to one Non-Commissioned Officer (NCO) and twenty Other Ranks (OR).

On 12 September 1897, 10,000 Pashtuns attacked the signalling post at Saragarhi, so that communication would be lost between the two forts.

What happened next was a tremendous tale written in blood by twenty-one Sikh warriors against 10,000 barbaric Afghan warriors in defending Saragarhi and not giving up in spite of a brutal death staring at them. All they had to pull through the battle was their attitude, grit and determination. Led by Havildar Ishar Singh, the Sikh warriors killed close to 450 Afghan warriors till the reinforcement arrived at Saragarhi.

This battle is celebrated even today by the Sikh regiment on 12 September every year as the Regimental Battle Honours Day, and is considered as one of the epitome of last stands.[21]

The Battle of Saragarhi is about the attitude of never giving up and taking a stand confidently, even when death breathes foul on your face.

A sportsperson and a soldier have many things in common and one of them is for sure the responsibility they have on their shoulders towards their country. Hailing from a defence background and having the privilege of knowing few national-level sports personalities very closely I can safely say they have a common character of not letting their country down. It is almost like an attitude or a sense of superiority where nothing matters more than the pride of their country, which they take very seriously.

---

[21]https://en.wikipedia.org/wiki/Battle_of_Saragarhi

Saina too has been raised with an attitude of utmost respect for the game and the country. She has grown up with tremendous self-belief and a stubbornness to not accept defeat. Anything she does is always with the ultimate vision of glory and a strong desire to win.

T.S. Sudhir has written that in the early years of her career Saina was on the receiving end of her seniors. They would complain against Saina's extremely aggressive approach on the court and the fact that she showed no respect towards them outside of it, but was quite indifferent to them. Often her introvert nature and the contrasting aggression on court were perceived as arrogance and a heady attitude.[22]

But these things did not bother Saina because in her mind she was on a different journey, one where these complaints were not even a consideration.

Winning Attitude

Saina has always approached courts with aggression and a tremendous belief that she can win, self-doubt is not really her forte. As mentioned earlier, even during her lean patch in 2010 and 2011 when she was struggling with her form, many thought that she has peaked her career and does not have much to offer to the game, but the iron-willed lady had other plans. She took her time to figure out her foothold and stand up again. But once she did, she brought glory to the

---

[22]Sudhir, T.S. 2012. *Saina Nehwal: An Inspirational Biography*. Nimby Books/ Westland.

entire country with a bronze medal in the London Olympics.

LEARNING TIP

With the right attitude,
you can fulfil dreams of massive amplitude.

If you look at professional world, majority of professionals suffer from misplaced priority towards money and designation and develop an attitude accordingly. In fact this approach of 'what is in it for me?' has spread to epidemic proportions. If you look at Facebook, Google, Tesla, or closer to home—Infosys, you'll see that the attitude of its founders was not driven by money but with the cause of changing the face of technology. It is a different matter that what followed was El Dorado, the city of gold.

From a discussion perspective, for any professional to be successful he needs to have the right attitude. This right attitude is maintaining utmost honesty and commitment to your work with a strong desire to learn. More often than not you might not have answers to a lot of questions, but the right attitude is to go out and find those answers, and that is how you become the winner.

Confidence

Every sportsman some time in his or her life has to make a choice between studies versus sports. Statistics reveal that out of every four students who excel in sports, three of them decide to withdraw themselves from it during high school.

Saina too was confronted with a similar challenge once she started participating in badminton competitively and after a fair amount of consideration post her intermediate, she discontinued her education. This was not an easy decision for her to make. It took plenty of introspection, discussion with parents and assurance from her coach Gopichand to come to a conclusion that badminton was her future. But once the decision was made there was no looking back. With a firm grip on her emotions and badminton racquet in her hand, Saina marched towards her future and went on to win every possible match till she became the world champion.

This incidentally is a very important quality of all the famous personalities in the world: the ability to back one's decisions and confidently work towards achieving their goals. Many critics in textbook style call it a gamble, but many optimists in textbook style call it confidence and that is the reason Saina Nehwal has won twenty-one career titles (see the table on the following page).

Saina Nehwal's winning record in Super Series finals

	Year	Tournament	Opponent	Country	Score
1	2006	Philippines Open	Julia Wong Pei Xian	Malaysia	21–15, 22–20 [57]
2	2008	Chinese Taipei Open	Lydia Cheah	Malaysia	12–21, 21–18, 21–9
3	2009	India Grand Prix	Aditi Mutatkar	India	21–17, 21–13 [58]
4	2009	Indonesia Open	Wang Lin	China	12–21, 21–18, 21–9 [59]
5	2010	India Open	Wong Mew Choo	Malaysia	20–22, 21–14, 21–12 [60]
6	2010	Singapore Open	Tai Tzu-ying	Chinese Taipei	21–18, 21–15
7	2010	Indonesia Open	Sayaka Sato	Japan	21–19, 13–21, 21–11
8	2010	Commonwealth Games	Wong Mew Choo	Malaysia	21-19, 21-23, 13-21
9	2010	Hong Kong Open	Wang Shixian	China	15–21, 21–16, 21–17
10	2011	Swiss Open	Sung Ji-hyun	South Korea	21–13, 21–14
11	2012	Swiss Open	Wang Shixian	China	21–19, 21–16
12	2012	Thailand Open	Ratchanok Inthanon	Thailand	19–21, 21–15, 21–10
13	2012	Indonesia Open	Li Xuerui	China	13–21, 22–20, 21–19
14	2012	Denmark Open	Juliane Schenk	Germany	21–17, 21–8
15	2014	India Grand Prix Gold	P.V. Sindhu	India	21–14, 21–17

16	2014	Australian Open	Carolina Marín	Spain	21–18, 21–11
17	2014	China Open	Akane Yamaguchi	Japan	21–12, 22–20
18	2015	Syed Modi International	Carolina Marín	Spain	19–21, 25–23, 21–16
19	2015	India Open	Ratchanok Intanon	Thailand	21–16, 21–14
20	2016	Australian Open	Sun Yu	China	11–21, 21–14, 21–19
21	2017	Malaysia Masters	Pornpawee Chochuwong	Thailand	22-20, 22-20

Source: Wikipedia

Saina Nehwal's runner-up record in Super Series finals

	Year	Tournament	Opponent	Country	Score
1	2007	India International Challenge	Kanako Yonekura	Japan	13–21, 18–21[61]
2	2011	Malaysia Masters	Wang Xin	China	21–13, 8–21, 14–21[62]
3	2011	Indonesia Open	Wang Yihan	China	21–12, 21–23, 14–21
4	2011	Super Series Masters Finals	Wang Yihan	China	21–18, 13–21, 13–21
5	2012	French Open	Minatsu Mitani	Japan	19–21, 11–21
6	2015	All England	Carolina Marín	Spain	21–16, 14–21, 7–21
7	2015	World Championships	Carolina Marín	Spain	16–21, 19–21
8	2015	China Open	Li Xuerui	China	12–21, 15–21

Source: Wikipedia

A few things are quite evident if one looks at her winning record above carefully:

1. As Saina gained confidence she started winning more international titles. In fact if statistics were to speak, she won approximately 3–5 titles a year from 2009 to 2012 which shows the kind of prime form she was in. The interesting bit is that, with an exception of 2011, the year when her performance was clouded the most owing to a ligament injury and coaching issues, she won just one title. Besides that year, she has dominated a sport for which China is better known. Her good form continued through 2012–14 as well, however, since then injuries have affected her performance.
2. If we look at the opponents' country-wise winning record of Saina, you will notice that she has won the maximum number of titles (5) against Chinese players. Before we move forward a bit of background about the badminton talent programme in China is necessary. Unlike India, China has a very organized development programme for its players where the talent is identified and trained from as early as three years of age, they are groomed and provided organized support till they become a global talent and start winning medals for the country. In light of the above fact, Saina's success becomes more plausible, purely because in contrast to the Chinese, Saina is a product of a relatively unorganized set-up, and Indian players have not really been known to perform well against their Chinese counterparts. But this situation took a turn for the better since Saina's

arrival on the international scene.

3. Second in her list of maximum titles won against are Malaysian players (4), who again are considered to be a very strong competition on the badminton court.

Some of the observations from her runner-up record are:

1. The years 2008, 2009 and 2010 were the golden phase of Saina's career. If she made it to the final match of a tournament she always emerged as the champion.
2. In 2011, she faced Chinese players in three finals and lost to them on each occasion. However, this can be discounted knowing that she was injured that year and was up against tough competition. On the contrary the plausable fact is that even though she was injured that year, she was still the runner-up in several of those tournaments.

Badminton is an individual sport, and based on the players' rankings allows multiple representation from the same country, thus increasing the competition in each international series organized. Yet, to have won twenty-one Super Series titles and be the runner-up in eight others is a commendable job and which could not have been possible without the confidence Saina has in her game.

As discussed earlier, when S.M. Arif saw Saina practicing in Lal Bahadur Shastri Indoor Stadium for the first time, he was very impressed with the way Saina conducted herself and approached the game. Seeing her he made a prediction that she is going to be a force to reckon soon, such a bold prediction for a girl who was barely eleven spoke a lot about the quality of her game.[23]

Slowly and steadily, Saina started proving S.M. Arif's prophecy true. Early on she started making an impression on the court by dominating her age group to a point where her coaches started pegging her against players much older to her. She justified the confidence of her coaches, participating in the senior category tournaments she gave a tough fight to players who were almost twice her age and brought many on their knees.

Saina Nehwal's winning record in national finals

	Year	Tournament	Age group	Her age	Format	Score
1	2002	Sub-Junior National Badminton Championship	Under-13	12	Singles	11–0, 11–4
2	2002	Sub-Junior National Badminton Championship	Under-13	12	Doubles	11–5, 11–4
3	2002	Sub-Junior National Badminton Championship	Under-16	12	Doubles	11–2, 11–3
4	2003	Sub-Junior National Badminton Championship	Under-16	13	Singles	11–3, 11–13, 11–2

[23]https://umasudhir.wordpress.com/2010/06/29/the-world-at-sainas-feet-well-almost/

5	2003	Sub-Junior National Badminton Championship	Under-16	13	Doubles	15–6, 15–7
6	2004	Junior National Badminton championships	Under-19	14	Singles	11–2, 11–4
7	2004	Junior National Badminton championships	Under-19	14	Doubles	15–6, 15–10
8	2005	Junior National Badminton championships	Under-19	15	Singles	11–5, 13–10
9	2005	Junior National Badminton championships	Under-19	15	Doubles	15–2,15–4
10	2007	Senior National Badminton Championships	Senior	17	Singles	21–19, 21–16
11	2007	National Games	Senior	17	Singles	24–22, 21–15
12	2008	Senior National Badminton Championships	Senior	18	Singles	21–11, 21–10

Source: Wikipedia

If you look at her performance in the table above you would realize that she had the confidence to win right from an early age. Below are a few takeaways from the table:

1. Even as a twelve-year-old, Saina participated in categories much beyond her age group. She was comfortable in playing in under-13 and under-16 categories, winning both the single and doubles title in the former and doubles

title in the later.

2. In 2004 and 2005, while she could have participated in under-16, she consciously decided to participate only in under-19 categories and won in both singles and doubles titles.
3. In 2006, when she was all of fifteen she started participating in the senior category title but lost to then reigning national champion, Aparna Popat. Besides that loss, she almost dominated the scene in the senior category as well.

In 2005, when Saina was the national junior champion, she played against the then National Champion Aparna Popat in finals and lost. Jamshedpur saw a fifteen-year-old champion in the making battling it out against a strategically deft twenty-seven-year-old nine-time national champion. This defeat, however, did not break Saina's spirit and in her trademark stubborn attitude she decided it was time to shake things up. And nine months later, both the players were standing against each other again in Asian Satellite Badminton Championship organized in New Delhi in October 2005. Saina Nehwal defeated Aparna Popat in straight games 11–8 and 11–6 to win the title.[24]

■

[24]http://www.firstpost.com/sports/from-hunter-to-hunted-saina-nehwals-big-predicament-1703839.html

Out of the sports arena in India, another personality who often epitomizes confidence and self-belief is the superstar of the millennium, Amitabh Bachchan. Film or non-film fraternity, he commands amazing respect across.

When he started his career, he was only at the end of rejections for being too tall for films. Many suggested that he try for a presenter's position with the All India Radio because of his heavy baritone, but he didn't even qualify for its audition. However, he did not give up hope and soon *Saat Hindustani* happened, but after this whiff of air there was a prolonged silence till *Anand* and *Zanjeer* happened two years later. Decades later, when he forayed into business with his film production and event management company—ABCL, things did not go the right way and he ended up bankrupt. Down but certainly not out, he waited for the right opportunity till *Kaun Banega Crorepati* happened, and the rest as they say is history. He had confidence in himself and did not let difficult situations play havoc with him.

At this point I recall these famous words by Dale Carnegie:

Inaction breeds doubt and fear. Action breeds confidence and courage. If you want to conquer fear, do not sit home and think about it. Go out and get busy.

LEARNING TIP

Have confidence in yourself, it's a rare commodity which not many can afford.

And this is something which every professionl should aim at—having such a deep understanding of one's skill, that you have attitude to deal with any situation in life, because as one moves forward in life, there may come occasions when things might not go right but it is only confidence and willpower that will help you pull through such periods.

Passion

Many a times I wonder what goes in the mind of a sportsperson. After a fair amount running into walls, I found an answer from a former national-level badminton player. According to her, sportspersons are no different from other human beings. 'We, like others, have our own worries, but when on court the winning attitude and a desire to be the best fades the rest into faint negligible noises,' she explained. This is also exactly what an acquaintance, the CEO of a reputed company, had told me. To put it in his words, 'Mr Gupta, we like any other person are human beings. And yes, life happens to us as well, in my case it's just that I have decided to not get affected by it and be focused on my career.' Probing further when asked about work-life balance, pat came an expected reply from the gentleman, 'For me this is not my profession, this is my passion.' While statements like these can be disputable from the point of work-life balance, still, such people are a dedicated lot for whom their passion is their winning mantra—much like Saina. This also brings us to a widely debated point among the neo generations, 'passion vs profession'. As we know, Saina decided to choose badminton over studies as her profession, a wise choice, since we know what she has done for the game and the country. But from an average Joe's perspective it is a tough choice to make.

However, I sincerely believe a successful person is just another average person who was aware of his potential and was determined to go forward with passion and hard work. In other words:

Successful person = Average person + Self-awareness + Passion + Hard work

Now let's evaluate the above equation and analyse what is missing there. While the above equation does take care of internal variables, it does not talk about external variables like getting a chance to perform, right platform, etc. To represent the external variable, let's use the word opportunity. So, working further on the equation above:

Successful person = Average person + Self Awareness + Passion + Hard work + Opportunity

Many might say these are easy words to write, but tough to implement. Yes, that is right and that is where passion and hard work come in. To prove a point, here I would like to plug a story from our neighbouring country, China. This is the story of a businessman named Jack Ma, who went on from earning $150 a year to earning close to $11 billion a year.

After the former US President Richard Nixon visited Hangzhou in 1972, Ma's hometown became a tourist spot for many. As a teenager, Ma started waking up early in morning to visit the city's main hotels, offering English-speaking visitors tours of the city in exchange for English lessons.

He was not the brightest of the students, failing in many subjects at school. Despite his persistence to get into the best college in the city, he failed twice only to be accepted by an average college the third time. In fact he applied to Harvard University ten times and was rejected each time. Like any other student after his graduation, Jack Ma was faced with the challenge of competing with his batchmates to secure a good job with a decent salary. A college degree in English from a not-so-great college certainly didn't work in his favour.

He applied to thirty different jobs and was rejected by all of them. In an interview with Bloomberg, he even confessed that out of twenty-four candidates, he was the only one who was turned away for a position at KFC. When he applied for a post in the police department, he was told that he was physically unfit for it. Being good at spoken English, all he could manage were short teaching assignments in various universities.

In 1995, Jack Ma travelled to the US for his translation business. Impressed with the way American economy was capitalizing on the Internet, he tried his hand with online search by searching for beer and was surprised to know none of the Chinese brands turned up over there. Intrigued, he decided to set up an Internet company for China. After few initial hurdles and a lot of persistence, he along with seventeen of his friends started Alibaba.com to build it into a company with a net worth close to $200 billion.

Jack Ma's life was not all rosy with everything falling in place itself. He had more than his fair share of rejections, in fact so many that an average Joe would have given up. But for him, his failures were his success mantras. His attitude of never giving up gave him unparalleled experience in how not to do things and prepared him for the big stage.

Opportunities come knocking on doors for a select few, the rest of them have to create it for themselves. In a very interesting article written in *Forbes* magazine, noted author and contributor Dan Schawble has said that the most important trait of successful people is they make their own luck:[25]

> They know that they make their own luck. Luck is derived from hard work over time and positioning yourself for success. You won't randomly get lucky and successful people know that. They will do at least one thing every single day to put themselves in a better position to get lucky and then use that luck to grow.

LEARNING TIP

A hard-working and persistent average Joe is what successful people are made of.

---

[25]https://www.forbes.com/sites/danschawbel/2013/12/17/14-things-every-successful-person-has-in-common/#58f829983c74

Successful people are seen as extremely self-confident, but the truth is they are just regular people like you and I, who have studied their skillset so well that they are masters at it.

The road to success is often less travelled, because the country miles in this journey are far lesser than the road block one faces. But hey, as they say: 'No pain, no gain.'

As for Saina, she never sat on her abilities thinking she will be discovered some day and will become an international star. For her it was a long journey of trials, tribulations, hard work and self-discovery, where things did not always go smooth. Instead, what it took was a lot of sweat, commitment, and above all her passion to win.

Even now when she has achieved so much in her life and can easily rest on her past laurels, every morning she gets up with the same level of enthusiasm and dedication which she had as a child and hones her badminton skills for at least 6–7 hours. This is the attitude all leaders and winners must have, irrespective of the field they are in.

For Saina, it is always about being prepared for that next match she would be playing. The Roman philosopher Seneca once said, 'Luck is what happens when preparation meets opportunity'—and that stands true for all winners.

An Analytical Mind: The Game Changing Trait

> True battle rages inside. It is not on the field that the battle is won, but in the mind.
>
> —Fleetwood

Have you watched the 2011 critically acclaimed movie *Moneyball*, directed by Bennett Mill? It's a story revolving around a baseball team coach (Brad Pitt), who sets out to rebuild his team with the help of an unconventional approach designed by a Yale University economist (Jonah Hill). The approach involves assessing the players beyond their star value to draft the best possible team and making it to the finals of that baseball season. The movie is a fine example of how being analytical pays off in sports.

Closer to home, Rajasthan Royals, the winning team of the inaugural IPL in 2008 went down in history as a similar example. A meagre $67 million team, Rajasthan Royals were pegged as underdogs right from the beginning due to lack of star power and experienced players. Captained by Shane Warne and supported by the team psychologist Jeremy Snape, what followed that season was magic and a classic example of the importance of being analytical and applying oneself well on the field.

Being analytical is not science or a mathematical equation, it is more of an approach based on past experiences and data to device a sound counter strategy in dealing with people and situations. It is one of the most important arsenals, but using it effectively in the right situation is subject to one's interpretation.

People with strong analytical skills are not born different, nor are they endowed with special abilities. They are just a set of people who like to identify patterns in situations and try to devise a mechanism to counter similar issues whenever they arise in the future.

Saina in many ways reflects such traits in her game. While she is aggressive as a player on the court, she is also constantly thinking and altering her strategy depending upon her opponents and their moves.

In this chapter, the word analytical will often be replaced with the word strategy, because the outcome of being analytical is devising strategies to deal with the subject in question.

What is being analytical?

The word analytical is derived from the Greek word 'analysis' which means, deconstructing things to identify its essential elements, often to serve a parallel purpose, which in Saina Nehwal's case is devising a sound counter strategy for her opponents.

Being analytical in any sport is very important, just like a brain in a body, it is the base on which mentally the entire match is played in advance. At times, the importance of being analytical is undermined in sports, but at the highest level of competitive sports where fitness levels of players are almost at par, it is the strategy and level of preparedness which makes the difference while scoring the winning points.

Badminton although is an individual sport, the importance of being analytical can't be discounted here either. In fact, there is much more analysis and thinking involved in badminton when compared to any team sport. While there is collective intelligence involved in team sports, games like badminton have only one person thinking on his feet. To add to it, the fast-paced nature of the game does not make things any easier either.

Imagine you strategizing your next move while shuttles are being hurled towards you at a speed of 200+ km/h. Sounds tough? How about some cheering crowd around expecting you to deliver the goods in the match? And on top of all that, how about the expectation of an entire nation on your back? I can see a realization dawning on the faces of quite a few who think only a game of cricket or football needs analysis or strategy.

Believe me when I say it is not easy being there—emotions, pressure, expectation, hostile crowd, taxing travelling schedules, time zones, alien food, and last but not the least strong competition add up to more than what one bargains for. To keep yourself sane and strategize at a micro level under such taxing circumstances, is anything but easy.

In his book, T.S. Sudhir has written that Gopichand admitted that Saina was not a natural player and that most of her shots have been honed over a time period of twelve years; but once a coach teaches her an interesting strategy or stroke, she will practice it hard and execute it in the most critical situations. This, I feel, is one of the most important traits of a world-class player—to practice diligently and deliver when most important.[26]

Unlike a game of cricket, where the game stretches across nine hours or five days, in the game of badminton at times the entire match gets over in a matter of minutes (a match can last anything between half-an-hour to one hour) and in such a scenario it is very important to judge a player's match strategy against their real style and readjust once own strategy.

On the art of playing in crunch matches, a former national-level badminton champion says, 'Basically, it is a lot happening on the court. You have to adjust your strategy

---

[26]Sudhir, T.S. 2012. *Saina Nehwal: An Inspirational Biography*. Nimby Books/ Westland.

from serve to serve to ensure that the opponent's move is neutralized. It is all about who runs out of steam first.'

While the primary ammunition in a game remains focus, strategy and analysing the opposition's game on computers and other tools, designing a counter strategy against them is equally important. In Saina's case, each match has a pre-match strategy which is finalized between her and her coach and is put to execution by her.

Contrary to Saina's preferred aggressive style of playing, at times the game is required to move in a different zone in order to get the desired results.

For instance, if a player whose original style is to score points quickly through tactics like smashes and drop shots realizes that the other player is exhausted but equal to his/her tactics, the game is taken into overtime with rallies to tire them out.

Badminton, in principal, is all about scoring and not letting the other person score, it's a constant tussle of being one up over the opponent.

If one sits down to analyse badminton, or for that matter any other racquet sport, they will then come across the five golden rules to be effective in this sport. I have elaborated these in detail below.

1. Vary your strategy according to your opponent

No two players have the same match strategy. While one might be a very good net player feeding on the patience of a player, the other could be an aggressive one sapping him/her out with their smashes. It's important for a player of

Saina's calibre, to be analytical enough to understand both situations and adjust her game to deal with them.

One instance where a young Saina amply demonstrated this side of hers, which I categorically remember, is the Indonesian Open in 2009. Saina Nehwal did not start as the favourite in the championship. Each match she played was before a packed stadium full of upbeat noisy crowd. Her semi-final match was against Lu Lan of China. Known for her aggressive game, Lu Lan fought it out for each point with Saina. Giving Lu a taste of her own medicine Saina retaliated against every aggressive move of Lu. Before a surprised Lu could realize what hit her, she lost the match to Saina by 25–23 and 21–19. There was a short phase in the match where it looked like Lu would win, only to be later surprised by a gritty Saina.

In the finals, she faced another Chinese player—world no. 3, Wang Lin. Wang's style of playing was very different from Lu's, and Saina took some time to understand that. But once she got a hang of the craftiness being used by the Chinese player, she started fighting back with raw aggression. The trick worked and Wang was thrown off track. Saina won 12–21, 21–18 and 21–9 to lift her first ever Super Series title. In fact, the first ever by any female Indian player.

LEARNING TIP

Being nimble with your strategies is the key to succeeding. One size never fits all.

What one needs to understand is that in one's professional life the concept of 'one size fits all' does not exist. Even in professional world, one needs to adjust their strategies from client to client, individual to individual and situation to situation. A classic example of this is Ratan Tata. The mild-mannered former Chairman of the Tata Group of Industries while very soft-spoken and down to earth, was also known for his analytical mind and strong ability to strategize. It was under his leadership that Tata group grew by leaps and bounds, becoming one of the biggest corporate houses in India. While he was known to have implemented some of the most important employee-friendly policies, he never shied away from raising an axe on anything which was associated with non-performance. Whether it was shutting down certain units of the group or acquiring ailing businesses like Jaguar and Land Rover, Ratan Tata is the reason Tata group is where it is.

Many think being analytical in sports is an outward process of strategizing against the opponents, however this is not the case. Being analytical is a two-way process, in sports while it is important to analyse and strategize against opponents—it is also important to indulge in introspection and devise necessary corrective measures, everything that is covered in training. It is this continuous process of honing skills based on one's own analysis and of their coaches which produces world-class talent.

Talking about the professional world, almost all the executives besides having a hawk-eye on their business and competitors, undergo the churn of self-evaluation and constant conversation with one's self to have a hang of where they score and where they need to improve.

Digging deeper, if one has to lay a process around self-evaluation they can follow the following steps:

- Talk about your long-term career plans. One needs to have clarity about what he or she wants to do in long-term. The course of one's self-evaluation is decided once he/she identifies where they want to be at the end of their career i.e. is it success or more of a work-life balance?
- Set regular checkpoints to measure your performance against the long-term goals. It is very important to have checks and balances against the set goals to ensure course corrections whenever necessary.
- Learn to ask hard questions. Failure is always a possibility, it is not always going to be that you achieve the set targets, one needs to be comfortable enough to ask probing questions and find a resolution to them.
- Devise strategies to handle shortcomings. There are going to be times when solutions to certain issues would be long-term and until then those issues would be visible as glaring shortcomings to others, in such situations not having a quick fix to the issue is not a solution. One needs to find a way to work around the situation till the cause of those issues is fixed permanently.
- Ask for training, guidance and mentoring. We have

discussed about this earlier, but in a professional world you would not have solutions to all the issues. In such scenarios taking help of others would be equally important.

- Re-evaluate your long-term plans to reset them according to the external factors. Many a times we under/overestimate ourself, in such scenarios it is always advisable to again take a hard look at the long-term goals and course correct.

2. Being aggressive

Saina Nehwal, in the badminton fraternity, is known for her aggressive game and strength. But what many ignore is that it is a part of Saina's winning strategy. She is known for doing a thorough homework before every match.

From a professional perspective, imagine you being a fresher and newly inducted in a company to be a part of their sales team. Your manager, after the induction, assigns you to go on a sales pitch with one of your new clients. Like a thorough professional, you do your research about your client and the kind of products that could be pitched to him based on your manager's inputs. With the analysed data you develop a list of expected counter questions and prepare well for them. As you enter the room, your client sees you as a person who is still ambling between boyhood and manhood pitching for his company. The meeting starts with a very low expectation as the client thinks you have not seen enough sunsets to justify your presence in the room, but what takes him by surprise is the in-depth knowledge you possess about your company products and the requirements he has. Question by question your appearance is nullified by your knowledge and the deftness with which you reply him back. Soon you have made your first kill and the client gives you the business.

While the above might read like a scene from a movie, Saina has gone with this level of preparedness in every match she has ever played. Even as a twelve-year-old, she surprised opponents much older than her with her prowess—and all this cannot be achieved with just aggression. You need to have a thinking mind that is alert enough to constantly analyse the opponent's moves and adjust the game accordingly in favour.

Badminton in terms of style and pace is very different from say lawn tennis or cricket. It involves aggressive movements, long shots, high shots, fine placements, soft drops, fatigue factor and occasional grunts with fist pumping coming into play. Majority of the strategies and analysis breathe and thrive within these boundaries and players use them to their advantage.

Just like sports, professional world also does not appreciate aggression while planning. When on the planning table the focus should be on strategizing how to defeat the opponents in mind games. However, when it comes to execution of those plans aggression seeps in and plays a very important role to make sure the goals are achieved.

Usually, it is the sales team of a company that shows the most aggression, and anyone you meet from that particular discipline of a business will be very aggressive, working tirelessly to achieve their targets.

While sales teams by design are supposed to be aggressive, they are not the right example of what aggression is supposed to be like in the professional world, I usually regard them as a little overboard.

Any professional while preparing to achieve goals should compartmentalize their actions into planning and execution space. When I say planning, I usually mean over-planning, because playing the scenarios repeatedly in your mind and being fully prepared while executing them is the best space to be in, or in other words it gives you the leverage to be more aggressive while executing those goals. It is somewhat like practicing how to ride a bicycle as a child, it is only with repeated practice that you get a hang of how balance is managed.

LEARNING TIP

Aggression should be as well-planned as the plan itself. Unplanned aggression often backfires.

Aggression usually comes in while executing those plans. One should ideally know the tempo of his or her aggressiveness and plan his goal execution accordingly. While executing a group goal, assess various parts of the goal and identify in advance those pieces where you can support and volunteer for that part accordingly.

3. Look for the blind spot/weakness

As distasteful as it may sound, the fact remains that a major part of any player's winning strategy focuses on developing a plan on exploiting the weakness of their opponent. At the highest competitive level, where winning matters, it becomes very important to be prepared for a 360-degree counter attack and if necessary capitalize on the competition's weakness.

While thinking about capitalizing on the blind spot in badminton, one example that promptly pops up is that of the Danish badminton players. Denmark has been known to produce some of the world's finest badminton talent in all these years.

When Danish players started foraying into the world of badminton, to the rest of the badminton fraternity they came across as very strong players. After them dominating the global badminton scene for a couple of years, the Asian players finally managed to figure out the chink in their armour—their height. So, while the much taller Danish players were comfortable playing high shots, they were not comfortable dealing with low trajectory body shots as they had to bend their knees to deal with them. For the Asian players, soon a formidable foe became a tamable opposition.

Saina herself faced a similar situation where she was on the receiving end of rival players capitalizing on her weakness. But unlike Danish players, she fought back hard to change the course of the tide and emerge as the winner in the situation.

According to T.S. Sudhir, in the initial years of Saina

Nehwal's badminton career she had a weakness which a lot of her opponents capitalized on. She was known to be a strong opponent in the first half of a match, but if the opponent took the match to the third round their chances of winning against Saina increased manifolds. She, in sporting language, had issues with her stamina. While her stamina was enough to sustain at national-level matches, for international level she needed a different level of fitness.

Initially she lost few matches due to this drawback, but it did not take her much time to analyse what was going wrong and before things could spiral out of her hands she sat down with her coach Pullela Gopichand and devised a strategy to address the issue. With regimented effort and help from Gopichand, she focused on boosting her stamina levels to international standards and soon became a formidable opponent.[27]

LEARNING TIP

In the professional world external competition is like sports, capitalizing on blind spots is permitted. However, doing the same with internal competition could be detrimental and counterproductive.

In a more social set-up capitalizing a person's weakness may

[27]Sudhir, T.S. 2012. *Saina Nehwal: An Inspirational Biography*. Nimby Books/ Westland.

not be an admirable trait, but when you strategize for a sport or a war it makes a lot of sense. However, implementing the rule of capitalizing on a person's weakness in professional environment takes a different spin all together.

Competition in such an environment usually gets classified into external competition and internal competition. While dealing with external competition (usually companies and individuals outside his/her own company), the rules of the game are similar to as it is between sports rivals: you can strategize against their weakness to make sure that your company is benefited. While dealing with internal competition the equation changes and one has to make sure that the larger interest of the organization supersedes any kind of cut-throat competition.

Unfortunately in reality there are different schools of thought. While majority advocate ethics in managing internal corporate competition, few opine that it is alright to capitalize on a person's weakness. However, the ground reality is that majority of them actually blur the thin line while capitalizing on someone's weakness.

But what exactly is the right answer?

The fact is that an organization is like cogs of a machine. A well-oiled cog ensures that the other cog moves efficiently. In an ideal scenario, each resource should perform their own job to ensure that other person delivers his part. However, in the real world things can't be so mechanical. Feedback and guidance is required for any resource to improve and perform, but if the issue is impenetrable and a habit to an individual then there should be a professional resolution for the non-performing resource through organized feedback, performance improvement plans and evaluations to take a final decision. Bending the situation to your advantage is certainly not advisable. I have learnt in the professional world that 'karma exists and things do come full circle faster than one can imagine.' To ensure you have support of others in your difficult times, you should also be there for them when needed. Capitalizing on someone's weakness and moving forward by way of it does not exactly qualify as winning a fort.

4. Develop counter measures to neutralize their strength

The Chinese players are known to be exceptionally strong in professional badminton, in fact they dominate the game the world over. They are known for their tacit aggression, which means when on the court they do not shout like tennis players, but it is through their gestures that they flaunt their physical superiority. Almost taunting the opponent through their body language.

Imagine playing against such tough opponents in their own country and yet winning five Super Series against them. It certainly is no cakewalk. Saina's strategy to deal with the players from China was simple—give them a taste of their own medicine. So, each aggressive move of theirs was counter measured with an equally aggressive move from Saina's end.[28]

In any sport, players usually come in with multiple

[28] http://www.firstpost.com/blogs/saina-is-nothing-if-not-a-fighter-5447.html

strategies for each match/opponent. At times, depending on the counter strategy of the opponent they switch from one strategy to other. But if the opponent is equal to the counter strategies as well, the match usually rests on the player's quick thinking and the ability to improvise to neutralize the strengths of the opponent, which at the level of competitive sports happens in almost every 2nd game, and to survive and deliver in such circumstances one definitely needs something more than just aggression.

If we decode a match to granular level and try to derive the crux of any strategy, in most cases it will be not to play a winning shot every time, but to play a negotiating shot to win the game. Beyond sports, this fits true for most professions. For ease of understanding I will break it down to short-term and long-term interpretations of the statement.

From a short-term perspective, what it means is that an executive on each task assigned should look at it holistically. Doing a good job in the initial phase and not being able to take it to conclusion is not seen as a job well done. Aim should be to plan the project/assigned task in such a way that your signature should be visible across.

A classic example for executing a task perfectly right to the end is the former captain of the Indian cricket team M.S. Dhoni. Considered as one of the best inning chasers in modern cricket, in a face-off with tough targets Dhoni is known to maintain a consistent run rate till the 40th over of a match and accelerates from there on to achieve the targets. His aim is not to finish the match in the first 35–40 overs unless due factor or run rate is a consideration. He is brilliant at improvising his basic strategy depending upon the pitch and the bowler balling to him. Once he reaches the last lap, he accelerates and attacks the identified bowler to milk the runs.

Coming back to the long-term perspective, I believe being able to deliver the goods in the very first go in a professional scenario is usually very bleak, so one should not try to hit every ball out of the park, because after a point your game becomes predictable. Instead every professional should channel his or her energies in a way that ensures a successful career instead of short spurts of success.

One example which often comes to my mind in this context is of Sachin Tendulkar. In an international career of twenty-four years and over 34,000 runs, the Little Master at all levels has been an epitome of brilliance. Batting against some of the most formidable opponents, not only has he set the record of the highest runs in world cricket, but also delivered for his country on every occasion needed. His approach to his game and career was the same—performance with consistency!

With the advent of modern technology the way the players analyse opponents has changed dramatically. What used to be good old reel analysis once has been replaced with laptops and advanced software to study the opposition, the players, the design of their equipments and changes in their performance over time. Badminton Motion Analysis is one such software which can study the performance of players and give you details about the high and low points of oneself and the opposition, aiding you in making informed decisions about opponents.

LEARNING TIP

Whether it is short-term or long-term, the aim of an individual should be to develop sound counter strategy to achieve success.

Well, no matter how much the technology evolves the mind behind interpreting and synthesizing the information remains the same. Also, while the decisions are more informed, the experts devising the match strategy do not change and for sure those implementing the strategies in the court their face might change but the nature of pressure remains the same. Technology or no technology, the aim eventually is to neutralize the opponent.

5. Focus

The importance of focus in making a good strategy cannot be discounted. Many wonder why does one need focus in making a good strategy? The answer is simple, at the highest competitive level in sports and every sphere of professional life, the margin of visible error is blink-and-you-miss-it, and it is very important that the person observes the minutest detail of the opponent and spots errors made by them, which is impossible without focus and attention to details.

Saina, as mentioned earlier, is very analytical and observant. In her preparation for a game, she studies each and every move of the opponent until a counter strategy is devised. Also, while playing and post-match she makes a note of the key strengths of the opponent so that sound counter strategies are in place for future encounters.

From a professional world's perspective an example to illustrate the importance of focus while working towards a strategy would be that of the fall of Nokia Corporation.

In the late 1990s and early 2000s, the name Nokia was synonymous with anything which was related to mobile phones. People took pride in owning a Nokia phone, making it a darling the world over. However, over time, Nokia became overconfident about its product choice and what it offered to the customers. They stopped accepting the importance of innovation and kept pushing dated technology (read Symbian). Not acknowledging what was like a writing on the wall, they ignored a bevy of rising competitors standing at the cusp of horizon. Nokia's customers waited for their favourite to bounce back, but drunk in success and an out-of-focus Nokia fell short by a huge margin. In no time the likes of Apple and Samsung brought in cutting edge technology.

Assuming it to be a blip on the radar, Nokia decided to ignore what one could call a parallel world being created away from its universe. Soon other mobile phone companies started taking away Nokia's market share. What was probably one of the fastest changing markets in works, defining itself by constant influx of various technologies, design and mobile utility, Nokia could not comprehend the direction of the tide. Even before they could understand what had hit them, the likes of Apple and Samsung became the global leaders as it gasped for a breath of fresh air.

While it was over-confidence and lack of judgement which lead to Nokia's fall, it was the ability of Apple and Samsung to identify the cracks on the tough exteriors of Nokia that lead to the rise of two global giants which in present times define the future of mobile technology on earth.

Apple and Samsung probably did the smartest thing by playing around the rules of the industry set by Nokia, focusing on the existing technology of mobiles (Android) to develop world-class range of mobile phones.

As a professional, the ability to focus on your competition, to develop a skill which differentiates you from them, and at the same time being good at what others do is an art. Being able to always be a step ahead of your competition is what sets you apart.

I still remember a gentleman who used to work with me in one of the Big 4 consulting firms. An aggressive lad, he constantly asked questions and reasoned them out. It was almost as if he was out on a spree to get himself insulted. Soon I started observing a pattern in his conduct; he initially got himself beaten to ground on various concepts by experts in their respective fields, but soon started getting better at almost everything he had been put down for earlier. His strategy was to learn by challenging the best in the environment, to judge what his opponents were made of and build himself in the process.

LEARNING TIP

The delta between a good strategy and great strategy is focus. Attention to details makes all the difference.

While we considered him a pain, he very smartly and tactfully was decoding his opponents to build himself up and eventually that is what mattered. Irrespective of the field, if you want to excel then being analytical is very important. It is like the edge of a sword, making a person more effective and lethal. If applied on the fly, analytical skillsets can make a person slow in decision-making, however, if practiced well-enough and thought through in advance for certain repetitive situations, it can be extremely effective. For instance, the snipers in the defence forces have to undergo rigorous training to become ace shooters. Besides having top-notch fitness as a defence personnel, they have to be very sound in their understanding of target practice, for which they have to have a high degree of sensitization and knowledge of things like wind factor, density, curve, resistance effecting the trajectory of a bullet. All this might sound trivial to an amateur, but it has multiplier effect as the distance of the target from the shooter increases.

Initial practice involves numerous hours spent on honing their skills and shooting targets, but once they have a good understanding of how to execute a shot it is only a matter of measuring the basics and pressing the trigger of the rifle. Shooting becomes more like a second nature to them and they do not need hours of planning anymore to execute a shot. Simply put, the analysis bit of planning a gunshot becomes like a gut feeling for them, and that comes only with focus and practice.

In the professional world, in order to be effective in one's job, an individual must have a good understanding of the business and how things function in it, so that he or she has a strategy ready to deal with those normal situations and focus his or her energies only on those pieces which are new and imposing in terms of threat.

While being analytical is a very important element in dealing with situations and being prepared for the ones that may arise in future, drawing references and tethering to a thought process is not. There needs to be a fair bit of intuition in your approach and flexibility to consider options, else the results will be very specific and often not exceeding expectations. I call it weighing options and deciding the best course of action.

Be it sports personalities or successful professionals, strategy is one of the most important elements to their success. The way a player needs to devise an effective match strategy, similarly professionals across levels need to make a successful career strategy to keep themselves ahead of the competition.

I categorically recall the first couple of weeks of April

every year in the FMCD company I worked at earlier. The head of my department, a bright young man, would ask our team to devise a business growth strategy for our division. The first time he assigned me this responsibility he asked me to devise a plan on how I would give him X + 10 per cent growth figure in the following year. It had only been a year and a half since I had started working, I started shivering thinking what to present because according to me we were the soldiers and not the ministers. When I turned around and looked at my colleagues I realized that though some of them were just a year or two senior to me, they were at ease with the task and that was because they had been through the drill a few times before. Taking a control of my overwhelmed mind, I worked along with my seniors to figure the demons of growth and sales strategy.

LEARNING TIP

Being strategic is like having a map on the ship, without it one is at the mercy of the sea.

One thing I learned that day was that strategy is not the custodian of strategists; it is a way of life or the vision of an organization. In our case that was our individual sales strategy put together as a business growth strategy. In the two years I spent with the organization, there was immense learning I had in terms of how to strategize and work towards a common goal for the organization.

An important question which arises from the above discussion is that who is supposed to be a strategist in an organization? The answer is a resounding: 'All'.

Right from a leader to a junior-level professional, everyone in an organization is assigned goals to be achieved. While a leader might have to steer the entire ship, the people below have to make sure that the cogs running the rudder are well-oiled for the leader to steer the ship. The degree of responsibility might vary, but no one can take away the fact that it is still important that everyone performs as per the strategy designed for the success of the organization.

Saina is known for her strong analytical side, which comes in play very often. She is known to take each game on its merit. She has modulated her mind in such a way that everything between her and her matches is just white noise which she has learnt to tune out.

For any professional, it is very important to understand his or her profession and have clarity regarding the responsibilities—both operational and strategic. Designations should not decide the distance of your vision, because many a times one great idea planted in the right ear can give you a mileage far enough to make a career.

Brand Saina: Determination, Dedication and Hard Work

'Making promises and keeping them is a great way to build a brand.'

—Seth Godin

An interesting fact narrated to me as a child, which is also an example of what brand reputation does to your mind is that of the Great Gama. Born as Ghulam Mohammad Baksh, and popularly known as the Great Gama, he was an Indian wrestler born on 22 May 1878 in Jabbowal, a village in Amritsar. Awarded with the Indian version of the Heavyweight Championship 'Rustam-E-Hind' he was one of the most feared wrestlers of the early twentieth century.

Undefeated in a career spanning more than fifty-two years, he is widely considered one of the greatest wrestlers of all time.

Starting at an early age of ten, he was blessed with extraordinary strength and endurance. Just 5'8" tall, he in no time jumped ranks to be recognized as one of the best wrestlers in the country. At seventeen, he challenged the seven-feet tall Raheem Bakhsh Sultaniwala—the then Rustam-E-Hind. The match lasted less than an hour and ended in a draw, but established Gama as among the top three wrestlers in India at the time.

Soon he travelled to Britain to make a name for himself globally, but did not receive the warm reception he was accustomed to. The organizer of the World Championship turned him away saying he didn't qualify for the Championship due to his low height.

LEARNING TIP

A true brand transcends the time variable. It has the ability to become part of history.

An angry Gama went on and challenged the entire heavyweight wrestling fraternity that if anyone could avoid a pin down from him he would accept his defeat and go back to India. The first professional wrestler to take on his challenge was Benjamin Roller of America. In the bout, Gama pinned Roller in 1 minute 40 seconds the first time, and in

9 minutes 10 seconds the second time. On the second day, he defeated twelve wrestlers and thus gained entry to the tournament.

Soon Gama was pitted against World Champion Stanislaus Zbyszko—a formidable wrestler, whom the other wrestlers feared to contest against. However, Gama managed to make him hug the ground within the first few minutes of starting the bout and he stayed in that position for the rest of the three hours to nullify Gama's moves. Zbyszko, it is said, got so scared of that experience that he did not turn up the next day for a rematch and Gama was declared the winner by default. Gama and Stanislaus Zbyszko faced each other two more times in their careers, and each time Gama emerged victorious.

Time and again the Great Gama proved himself an undisputed winner in wrestling, in fact for eight years his title of Rustam-E-Hind went unchallenged. Even today, he is regarded as the father of Indian wrestling and his name is taken in the same breath as the other greats. Such is his brand that even now, whenever someone is blessed with superlative strength and wrestling prowess they are often refered to as 'Gama Pehelwan' out of love and respect.

While the story of the Great Gama illustrates how far-reaching a brand name can be, it also shows that a true brand goes beyond one's lifetime. If we look at Saina, she in many ways has achieved in the world of badminton what the Great Gama achieved for himself in the world of wrestling. In a country which is crazy about cricket and the scope for other sports at its best is far less, to first create a space for badminton and then command a substantial brand value to be acknowleded as an icon is not an easy task and takes more than determination to achieve it.

In India, over the years, Saina's name has become synonymus with badminton and her achievements are a dream for many.

Unpretentious and down to earth, she has never allowed arrogance to take over her achievements. Instead, she cherishes those who have supported her to achieve the dizzying heights where she sits humbly.[29] A doting child and a loving sister, Saina is well-aware of the sacrifices her family has made to make sure that she succeeds in her ambitions.

I have often wondered about what goes in the minds of successful people. To understand better what makes them succeed, I did a little research on few successful personalities. I found a common DNA knitting all of them together—focus and desire to succeed. Of course talent is important and forms the base of the monument, but to recognize it and work towards it religiously are the building blocks.

LEARNING TIP

While talent serves as the foundation, focus and desire to succeed act as the building blocks.

---

[29]http: / / www.vervemagazine.in / people / inspirational-icons-saina-nehwal-badminton-player

So, what defines brand Saina?

Aggression?

Simplicity?

Focus?

Hard Work?

Reliability?

Actually, it is a bit of all.

In business terms, Saina has been a product which has delivered beyond its parent brand to establish itself as an icon in her own rights. Somewhat similar to what Xerox did to photocopy industry.

In India, Xerox was the first company to introduce the photocopying machine. With time, as more shops installed Xerox machines it became a popular brand for the purpose. In fact there was a time when no other brand for photocopying would be seen in the shops and people started using the words 'Xerox' and 'photocopy' interchangeably.

LEARNING TIP

Aim for greatness, success will follow.

In the Indian context, it won't be too far-fetched to say that badminton has benefited from brand Saina and has made many Indians sit up and take notice of the sport. It is nothing less than a matter of pride for Saina when young, aspiring kids are asked what they want to be and they confidently say 'Saina Nehwal'. She has done for badminton what Sachin Tendulkar did for cricket, becoming a role model and illuminating a path less taken by others.

Saina has been the face of Indian badminton for long now and many brands have encashed on her success. Riding high on one such wave of her popularity is popular sports equipment brand Yonex.

Yonex has signed a special agreement with Saina under which the company manufactures 'Yonex GR 303 Saina Nehwal' brand of racquets, and as per the agreement with them 4 per cent profit from the sales of the racquets goes to her.[30]

Another company which effectively tied up with Saina was Sahara India. In 2012, Saina went ahead and signed a deal with Sahara to represent their brand. As a part of the deal she carried a logo of Sahara on her sports gear in all the international sports tournaments.[31]

Sharing platform with the likes of Lionel Messi, Saina Nehwal was declared as the brand ambassador of Huawei Honor mobile phones in India. Speaking about Saina representing Huawei as a brand ambassador, Allen Wang, President of the Huawei group said, 'Being brave requires courage, commitment and consistency which makes Saina a perfect fit for our brand. She truly exemplifies the Honor

---

[30]https://en.wikipedia.org/wiki/Saina_Nehwal#cite_note-CutRhitiSports-106

[31]https://sports.ndtv.com/badminton/saina-nehwal-signed-as-brand-ambassador-by-sahara-1543591

brand personality of 'For the Brave'.[32]

Capitalizing on similar sentiments, ITC group tapped into Saina's image for their Savlon brand of hygiene and antiseptic products, while announcing the association with Saina, Sameer Satpathy, Chief Executive, Personal Care Products Business, ITC Limited said, 'Savlon is happy to engage ace shuttler Saina Nehwal as the Brand Ambassador. Her journey truly exemplifies determination, dedication and hard work. Saina personifies Savlon's core brand thought of performance power in more ways than one'.[33]

Edelweiss group was another company which went ahead and tapped into Saina's brand image. Talking about Saina, Mr Rashesh Shah, Chairman & CEO, Edelweiss Group said, 'Saina is an inspirational icon widely recognized by people across all corners of India, which is one of the compelling reasons to associate with her. More than that, she's different—it is because of her that badminton is now watched by millions across our country. We have all seen her commitment to the game, her unwavering focus, sheer hard work and mental discipline as she keeps on getting better and better. [These are] all qualities that we at Edelweiss strongly identify with and constantly practice. It is indeed a pleasure to sponsor the champion, Saina Nehwal and have

---

[32]https://brandequity.economictimes.indiatimes.com/news/advertising/saina-nehwal-is-the-new-face-of-huaweis-smartphone-e-brand-honor/51625476

[33]http://www.exchange4media.com/Marketing/ITCs-Savlon-engages-Saina-Nehwal-as-brand-ambassador_65513.html

her as Edelweiss's brand ambassador.'[34]

Last but not the least, Kellogg's launched a master brand campaign starring Saina Nehwal. Resonating on sentiments captured by the other brands above, Harpreet Singh Tibb, marketing director, Kellogg's India said, 'Saina is young, ambitious, hard-working, a super athlete and a great role model for every young Indian. Plus, Saina had just achieved her dream of climbing to the world no. 1 spot in badminton and making India proud. So, she was a perfect fit for our campaign—'*Bade Sapno ki Sahi Shuruaat*' or 'Feeding Dreams'.[35]

The list is long, over the years many other companies like Top Ramen Noodles, Fortune Cooking Oil, NECC, Indian Overseas Bank, Vaseline, Deccan Chargers and couple of real estate and beauty products companies have also tied up with her effectively during different phases of her career, capitalizing on brand Saina.

Commanding an endorsement fee of ₹70–75 lakh per advertisement, her brand value received a major boost and shot up by 30–40 per cent to an endorsement fee close to ₹1.2–1.5 crore per advertisement the year she became the world no. 1.[36]

The Premier Badminton League franchise which was

---

[34]https://www.adgully.com/edelweiss-group-sponsors-saina-nehwal-and-signs-her-as-brand-ambassador-62880.html

[35]http://www.livemint.com/Consumer/nQZzGzlcg9TOZRDgLyfTpL/Kelloggs-rolls-out-masterbrand-campaign-starring-Saina-Nehw.html

[36]http://www.afaqs.com/news/story/45433_Saina-Nehwal-Smash-hit-for-brands

launched in India in 2013 brought the who's who of the badminton world to a common platform in India. Based on a model similar to Indian Premier League (IPL), PBL operates on the model of dividing the players into regional teams and organizing a tournament. In the inaugural round of this tournament Saina was the one who commanded the highest bid, fetching close to ₹60 lakh from Awadhe Warriors. She is the team's front-running player and has been retained by them consistently. For a marquee tournament like such, having Saina around ensures packed courts and plush sponsorships.

In 2013 and more recently in 2017, Saina Nehwal walked the ramp for designers like Pallavi Jaipur[37] and Neeta Lulla.[38] Accustomed to playing before packed stadiums, she confidently walked for the fashion shows as if she owned the ramp.

In 2012, the year Saina won the Olympics bronze medal her brand received a major boost. A year before, she had had a ligament injury in her right knee and was not sure whether she would be able to place her best foot forward. Until that bronze medal, she was considered a quality world-class player, but that Olympic win established her as a brand with resilience.

Saina has struggled with her injuries just the way Sachin Tendulkar did with his. While he was always the Master Blaster of cricket, there was a phase in his career

---

[37]http://www.goodtimestv.in/photos/saina-nehwal-walks-the-ramp-7684

[38]https://www.thequint.com/sports/sports-buzz/saina-nehwal-neeta-lulla-bangalore-times-fashion-week

when he could not perform his best because of his tennis elbow injury. His struggle with excruciating pain was even visible on the screen. Cricket fans all over the world were beginning to think that it was going to be the end of Tendulkar's career. But he had other plans; he fought back and made a star-like comeback. In fact many of his best performances came after he was treated for his injury—be it the first-ever double hundred in ODIs by any cricketer (2010) or helping India win its second World Cup (2011).

As a brand proposition it did something very interesting to Sachin's image, augmenting the variables it established him as a sportsman with the ability to go beyond pain and more importantly as a man with resilience towards adversities. This was followed by a series of advertisements which capitalized on this side of his personality, one specific advertisement which categorically sticks out is that of Adidas. The campaign had a punch line: 'Bring It On', and the video commercial started with the lines, 'It's a young man's game. He has to reinvent himself,' which was aptly captured the struggle faced by Tendulkar.[39]

In branding world, there is a concept called the product life cycle curve, which says every product goes through the four stages of introduction, growth, maturity and decline on a timescale variable. Similarly, every brand undergoes a life cycle known as 'brand life cycle'. Let us refer to the figures on the following pages for a better understanding.

[39]https://www.youtube.com/watch?v=ZUjIGVeAZSI&feature=youtu.be

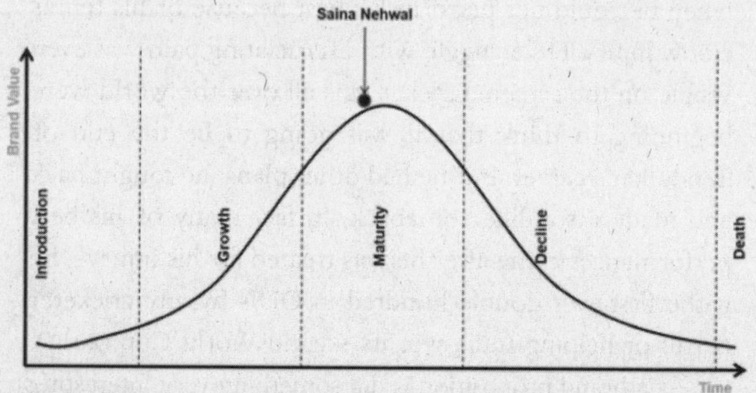

Figure 1: Brand Life Cycle

If you look at the Figure 1, you will see the four phases of a brand life cycle of Introduction, Growth, Maturity and Decline plotted adjacent on timescale variable (horizontal axis). What it means is that as time progresses and the brand performs it goes through the above mentioned phases of rise and fall.

One addition that I have made here is of innovating this concept further and introduced a fifth stage—death. I have done so because unlike a product, a living being undergoes an additional phase which is that of their death, and unless you are a legend like Don Bradman or Muhammad Ali, your brand power deteriorates to occasional recalls in conversations.

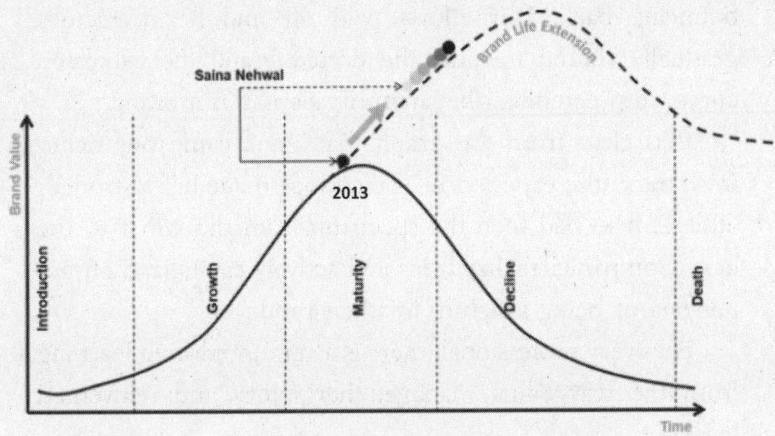

Figure 2 Brand Life Extension Curve

If you look at the curve in Figure 2, you will observe that in 2013 Saina was sitting at a very interesting juncture in the maturity phase of the brand life cycle curve, where advertisements were flowing in and she was the top performing athlete. But what followed was a spate of injuries in 2013 and 2014, which threatened to push her career towards a decline.

However, things took a turn in the right direction when she underwent treatments for the injuries. After a lean year during which she took time to rest and undergo an extensive treatment, she was back on the badminton court and rearing to go under the guidance of her new coach, Vimal Kumar.

Had Saina not reinvented herself, she could have begun slipping in her career. However, she never let the injury deter her and took the bull by the horns and worked towards bouncing back. Her efforts paid off and her trajectory gradually shifted towards the dotted brand life extension curve, thus extending her maturity period as a brand.

It is clear from the graph that Saina came out richer from the entire experience. The episode made her a stronger athlete, who had seen the spectrum from the worst to the best. Companies realized this and actively capitalized on her persona of being a fighter for their products.

For every professional, there is a very interesting learning from the way Saina managed her injury and reinvented herself.

Just like Saina, professionals from all spheres at times hit a wall in their career and growth prospects. In such times to make sure that the process of growth and evolution does not get stalled by any road blocks, they need to have an open mind to reinvent themselves and move forward.

LEARNING TIP

To stay relevant, it is important to reinvent one's self. Brands are about association and innovation–the New Age order for any company.

Let us take the example of the Western India Vegetable Products Limited, or more commonly known as 'Wipro'. Wipro was established by Azim Premji's father Mohamed Premji in late 1945. Incorporated with a vision to manufacture vegetable and refined edible oil, they focused on this core business till 1966. That year, after Mohamed Premji's death, his son Azim Premji returned to India from Stanford University and at the young age of twenty-one took over as Wipro's chairman.

Realizing that the company had the potential to go the distance and being limited to just edible oil business won't benefit them much, Azim Premji decided to diversify. Hence, began a journey of astronomical growth. Late 1960s and early '70s saw the company foray into other products like electricity bulbs, tubelights, packaged food, etc. In the '70s and '80s, the company shifted its focus to the IT industry which was still in its nascent stage. In the '90s, they shifted focus to specialized products and going into the medical industry under a joint venture with the General Electric group.

If Wipro had stuck to its core business, it is unlikely that it would have become the conglomerate that it is today. Azim Premji's vision and his company's willingness to constantly innovate is what paved the way for Wipro's success.

It is a coincidence of sorts that the year Saina Nehwal won the bronze medal in London Olympics she was presented with a BMW car by Sachin Tendulkar. I say coincidence because to me these are the two biggest names which come to my mind when we talk about brand life cycle extension in the sporting world.

■

Saina understands that as a public figure her followers like to have a window into her life and to make sure that she is accessible to the millions who love her you can find her on social media platforms like Facebook (8 million likes and 7.8 million followers)[40], Twitter (7.3 million followers)[41] and Instagram (almost 1 million followers).[42]

She uses these platforms not only to showcase a kaleidoscope of her personal and professional life but also to spread important public messages. A very important observation which one can't help noticing on these platforms is the simplicity which her social media account resonates, it is almost as if she maintains them herself.

A recent announcement for a motion picture on Saina Nehwal has got many excited. Critically acclaimed film-maker Amole Gupte will be directing the film, which will have actress Shraddha Kapoor play Saina's role.[43]

Saina was also among the top 100 celebrities in *Forbes* magazine's 2017 rankings. At the 29th position, Saina featured with earnings sum of ₹31 crore.

From 2009 to 2012 she was on what many call as the velvet patch of her life. Her performance was skyrocketing and so was her brand value. Every ribbon cutting event wanted her to do the honours.

---

[40]https://www.facebook.com/SainaNehwal.OGQ/

[41]https://twitter.com/NSaina

[42]https://www.instagram.com/nehwalsaina/?hl=en

[43]http://www.hindustantimes.com/bollywood/shraddha-kapoor-to-play-badminton-star-saina-nehwal-in-biopic-saina/story-NahchLkK3xGzqY3yJeLwrJ.html

■

Saina has dedicated herself to several social causes. In fact in 2015, she was named among the top twenty most charitable sports personalities in the world owing to her active involvement in various charities.[44]

Recently she showed her solidarity with the soldiers who protect our country and donated ₹6 lakh to the families of the twelve Central Reserve Police Force (CRPF) jawans who were killed in an encounter in Chhattisgarh's Sukma district.[45] While she does not believe in making noise about her charity work, one can often find her at various events across India supporting different causes.

Saina is also a firm believer in women empowerment. She makes it a point to interact with aspiring women and enjoys giving talks on various forums on the importance of women having careers and a will to win in life.

■

While Saina has achieved what only few can dream of, there is no dearth of critics who believe that badminton can never provide its players with star celebrity status the way cricket

---

[44]https://timesofindia.indiatimes.com/sports/off-the-field/Charity-begins-at-the-sports-field-for-these-athletes/articleshow/48639657.cms

[45]http://www.hindustantimes.com/other-sports/saina-nehwal-to-donate-rs-6-lakh-to-families-of-crpf-personnel-killed-in-sukma/story-JQCDy2xSMncbfZ827Usz3J.html

or tennis can. Saina understands this and for her performance and brand image are two sides of the same coin, and the long queues of the companies vying to sign her would disappear if she does not perform.

Saina's approach towards her game and her success often remind me of a saying by Henry David Thoreau, the American philosopher: 'Success usually comes to those who are too busy to be looking for it.'

She can be easily compared with leaders who tirelessly build the reputation of their company and in the process cements his or her position in the organization.

Badminton, especially women's badminton, to a great extent has gained momentum in India due to Saina's success. And now with the recent rise of more Indian female players like P.V. Sindhu and Rituparna Das, the future of Indian badminton surely is in strong hands.

The Great Gama of Indian badminton has risen and delivered beyond everybody's expectations of her. The next generation of badminton players will be faced with a legacy and brand that would be tough to match up to.

Leading a Successful Life: The Saina Way

'Most people chase success at work, thinking that will make them happy. The truth is that happiness at work will make you successful.'

—Alexander Kjerulf

Often we confuse happiness with success, thinking they are interchangeable, but the truth is that while happiness might be inclusive of success it does not necessarily mean it always has to be a part of it. An example would be Bill Gates.

When he was the world's richest man, he realized one day that just developing software was not enough for him—that it could never satisfy him completely. He decided to retire from Microsoft and plunge wholeheartedly into philanthropy with his wife, Melinda Gates. Together they set up the Bill and Melinda Gates Foundation with an endowment of US$ 44 billion. For the last seventeen years Bill Gates has been committed to this cause and intends to continue it.

Gates decided to dedicate his life to philanthropy because he had seen enough of the corporate world, whether it was his infamous rivalry with Steve Jobs or working hard to make Microsoft the no. 1 company in the world. He was just not into it anymore as his heart lay elsewhere. For a person like Bill Gates who had been there and done it all, such a decision might make sense. But what about those who have not achieved the epitome of success yet, those who are still climbing the ladder of success and yet have responsibilities in their lives?

Many a times, while contemplating about work-life balance I wonder how people with busy diaries manage their lives. How do their families deal with their professional schedules, the name and fame which comes along with it? How do they coordinate between their branding commitments and family commitments?

Still looking for answers, all I can say is that it is a complex maze—where one has to constantly shift focus between the aerial view of a happy family life and what lies ahead immediately, professionally as well as personally, to ensure the best of both the worlds.

In this chapter we would try to explore what drives Saina Nehwal in life and despite such unprecedented success how does she continue to be down to earth.

Her Success Mantra

Saina Nehwal, since early 2000s, has been extensively busy with international travelling, training, branding commitments and, if time permits, with social commitments and her family. Playing 10–12 tournaments on a yearly basis barely leaves any spare time in her kitty to dedicate it to other facets of her life.

As discussed earlier, even when she was injured during 2010–11 and 2013–14 many thought it was the end of her badminton career, but she proved her critics wrong and every time struck back with vengeance to win bronze medal in 2012 Olympics and coveted world no. 1 spot in 2015. It is almost as if she likes to prove people wrong, especially when she comes across as down and out. A firm believer in giving her best on the field, she has made it a mantra in her life.

Experts say, what Saina has been able to do in badminton is phenomenal. Usually, an international badminton player's shelf life is five to six years; but Saina keeping herself in prime form and delivering consistently at international platforms since 2008 is nothing less than extraordinary. An international career spanning over nine years, where she has been performing consistently is unbelievable to say the least. Case in point her recent gold medal in Gold Coast 2018, Commonwealth Games.

She loves to win and can invest herself to any extent

in making sure she does, it is second nature to her. Pullela Gopichand says:[46]

> I think individually—Saina has a huge drive to win, she's physically good, strong and a real worker on court.

A hard-working girl, Saina has been rewarded handsomely for her commitment to the game. Be it signing multi-crore endorsement deals or receiving the adulation of the entire country. Her never-say-die attitude and strong desire to win stand firmly behind her success and may be it is for people like her, John Calvin Coolidge Jr., the 30th President of the United States, once said:

Nothing in this world can take the place of persistence. Talent will not: nothing is more common than unsuccessful men with talent. Genius will not: unrewarded genius is almost a proverb. Education will not: the world is full of educated derelicts. Persistence and determination alone are omnipotent.

LEARNING TIP

Determination and hard work are the two most important pillars on which success hinges.

---

[46]http://www.firstpost.com/sports/saina-vs-sindhu-through-the-eyes-of-gopichand-1177839.html

Family

A daddy's girl, Saina has always drawn inspiration from her father. Having said that, Saina is very close to her mother as well, who has helped Saina in staying focused and keeping a reality check over her success and life.

When asked by a leading magazine about what she has learnt from her parents, Saina said:[47]

> Their confidence and self-belief. My dad always tells me: '*Himmat se khelo, jeetogey* (play with courage and you will win).' I have always followed this simple mantra.

As discussed earlier, Saina as a child always received encouragement from her parents for her endeavours, whether it was learning Karate or shifting her loyalties to badminton.

As a teenager she followed an intense badminton training schedule where she used to travel close to 24–25 kilometres at least twice a day for practice sessions at Lal Bahadur Shastri Stadium Hyderabad and had complete support from her parents in this quest. She has acknowledged that, 'The push from my parents was my strength. They have sacrificed a lot to help me reach where I am. Dad used to take loans from his friends to buy me racquets and pay for my coaching.'[48]

Saina is very respectful to her parents for the contributions

---

[47]http://jfwonline.com/article/saina-nehwal-talks-about-her-life-badminton-and-her-journey/

[48]http://jfwonline.com/article/saina-nehwal-talks-about-her-life-badminton-and-her-journey/

made by them in her life and may be that is the reason you can often see her getting emotional whenever someone talks about her parents' contribution in her success.

All this is history and Saina has brought her family a long way from those days. The fact that she earns in crores and has paid taxes worth lakhs over past few years shows she has boarded the rocket to the moon.

Her father, Dr Harvir Singh, Principal Scientist with the Directorate of Oilseeds Research in Hyderabad, takes pride in what Saina has achieved in her life. Soft at heart, his eyes moistens every time Saina makes him proud. While talking about his daughter's achievements at a symposium at the Indian Council of Agricultural Research, Pusa, Delhi, he said:[49]

> 'It is Saina who has made me, my work, community and my country proud. There isn't much more I can ask as a parent.'

When interviewed by one of the leading regional television channels of Telangana on the announcement of a Hindi film being made on Saina Nehwal, he said:[50]

> Till date I have read biographies of greats like Nehru and Gandhi, I never thought that someone would make a movie on my daughter and it is a feeling of elation that I would be seeing her story on the big screen soon.

---

[49]http://archive.indianexpress.com/news/saina-by-his-side-it-s-father-s-day-for-dr-harvir-singh-at-work/641149/

[50]Saina Nehwal's Father Harvir Singh Nehwal Exclusive Interview || Father's Day Special || || NTV https://www.youtube.com/watch?v=u89l1ulJSfU

A man with pragmatic approach in life, he initially wanted his daughter to be a doctor. But once he saw Saina blazing away in the world of badminton he decided to invest all his resources and energies in providing the right resources to his daughter. He says:[51]

> I do not think much about what I did for Saina, had she chosen studies as her interest area, I would have taken loans for her books and education as well, instead I think I invested that money in her career as a badminton player.

Saina is like a friend to her father and that is very evident from the camaraderie they share in the interviews and the photographs available on various social media websites. Her father admits that when it comes to dealing with Saina—between him and his wife, he is the calmer one and it is probably why Saina confides in him often. Saina credits the scale of her success to her mother, Usha Rani. She admits that her mother pushed her often and hard to go that extra mile. While badminton as a sport was introduced to her by her father, but it is the flight of her mother's dream that Saina carries in her eyes every time she steps on the court.

In Saina's professional life, while her father played the role of Rock of Gibraltar, her mother played the role of the guiding light—an essential combination of two people who

---

[51]'Har Ghar Kucch Kehta Hai'. Season 3, Episode 3—Saina Nehwal. Asian Paints. Published on 28 October 2015. https://www.youtube.com/watch?v=YdUOEE2bQFg&t=584s

celebrate every success and failure of their child as their own that everybody needs in their formative years.

There were times when Saina went soft, during those rare moments her mother made sure to pull Saina back and set the course right for her. From planting the Olympic medal dream to making sure her diet plans are religiously followed, she had a fair contribution in bringing out the champion in Saina, who admits:[52]

> Mentally, my mother is very strong, she and my father both used to play badminton and she is the one who has groomed me to be mentally so strong. She always told me 'Saina I want you to win a gold medal in Olympics.'

Firmly believing that sky is the limit, Usha Rani always inspires her daughter to not sit on her laurels. Setting the record straight, she said in one of the interviews:[53]

> I do not comfort myself on Saina's achievements, I always tell her to work hard and keep moving forward.

LEARNING TIP

A strong family support is a luxury for many. If you have it, you must appreciate it.

---

[52]'Walk The Talk' with badminton champion Saina Nehwal. NDTV. Published on 9 January 2015. https://www.youtube.com/watch?v=VnA5LRnwzVA

[53]'Har Ghar Kucch Kehta Hai'. Season 3, Episode 3—Saina Nehwal. Asian Paints. Published on 28 October 2015. https://www.youtube.com/watch?v=YdUOEE2bQFg&t=584s

Saina's relationship with her sister Abu Chandranshu Nehwal is typical of an elder and younger sibling. While Saina Nehwal was always the naughty child in the house, Abu Chandranshu was the ideal elder sister—shielding her from being at the receiving end of their parents for playing cricket with boys or for her pranks on Abu herself. As a child she made sure that Saina had a protective environment where she could flourish. A badminton player herself, Abu Chandranshu could not take her own game ahead due to asthma. The sisters share a close relationship and Abu Chandranshu has made sure to be behind Saina, supporting her every step of the way.[54]

Value Your Mentors

Saina has always been very close to her coaches, from P.S.S Nani Prasad and S.M. Arif to Pullela Gopichand and Vimal Kumar. Her coaches too, on their part, have always been very protective about Saina and have provided her the best possible support.

Saina realizes the investments made by her coaches in her growth and that is why she holds a very special mention of them in her life.

P.S.S. Nani Prasad, her first coach is the reason India got a badminton player like Saina Nehwal. The day the little hands of Saina hit her first smash in L.B. Stadium, it was 'Nani Prasad Sir' as Saina fondly calls him who saw the potential

---

[54]http: / /jfwonline.com / article / saina-nehwal-talks-about-her-life-badminton-and-her-journey /

in Saina and took her under his wings.

With the sincerity of a disciple she followed whatever Nani Prasad instructed her and soon Saina became a recognized name in the State-level circuit.

Saina is grateful to Nani Prasad even today, for setting a strong base for her. While she misses the presence of the departed soul in the success she has achieved, she does not forget to mention him whenever she talks about her journey to success.

Once Saina's association with Nani Prasad came to an end, she went under the guidance of S.M. Arif, the legendary coach who has the distinction of touching the professional life of almost all the current and past crop of national-level badminton players from India who have risen to global fame. A different make from Nani Prasad, he focused on Saina's endurance levels and strength. Saina continues to hold him in high regard, grateful to him for providing a strong physical base which helped her next coach Pullela Gopichand in carving out a global player out of Saina.

Saina stepped under Gopichand's wings in early 2000s. It did not take Gopichand much time to realize the potential in Saina. His own career cut short by a knee injury, Gopi still had a lot to prove and saw Saina as a medium through which he could live the rest of his badminton dreams.

What started then was a typical 'Guru–Shishya' relationship eventually led to Saina touching new heights every time she took a step forward. 'Gopi Bhaiya', as Saina refers to him, developed her game to a level where she soon started delivering the results.

Saina cherishes the relationship she shares with Gopichand and says he will always be the reason where she is. Her coach holds a very special space in her life and always has a fond mention in her conversations.

Once Pullela Gopichand was made the national coach, his responsibility towards the Tricolour increased manifold, focusing on the entire national team he could not spend as much time on her as both he and Saina would have liked. Saina too, while recovering from injuries, needed special attention and decided to train with Vimal Kumar in Bengaluru during the period. Kumar understood that more than anything Saina needed confidence and that is what he focused on, and soon she was on the road to recovery and started performing in the international scene.

After an association of three years during which Vimal Kumar played a role of a friend more than a coach to Saina, for the greater good of her game Saina decided to come back to Gopichand and SAI appointed Mr Mulyo Handoyo. This was a move which has been justified by her recent performance.

Irrespective whom she trains under, Saina has always been very humble with her coaches and has given them their due respect. Even at this point in her career where she can highjack all the limelight, she prefers to acknowledge her coaches whenever she can. Call it her upbringing or her mindset, she has always treated her coaches like demigods, the ones who have an equal right in claiming a stake in her fame and credentials.

Professionalism

Saina has a clear stance when it comes to her opponents. For instance, when quizzed about P.V. Sindhu in an interview, she said:[55]

> It is difficult to be friends with opponents. It is true that we train together and talk to each other every day. But we don't have the time to become good friends.
>
> We don't even have time to talk to our parents. Moreover, she is a big player now and an opponent to me. I am happy for her and wish that she does well. I know people are interested about our matches since both of us are Indians.

Sindhu too, in an interview to *Hindustan Times*, said:[56]

> We're friends, like hi-bye...and that's it. We actually play together during practice but there's not much time to get interactive and talk to each other because we have our training sessions, so there's no real time where we can sit and talk.

It is nice to see the two pillars of Indian badminton being on a good stead while bringing glory to the country, but as a player it highlights another important aspect of Saina's—

[55]https://timesofindia.indiatimes.com/sports/badminton/Saina-Nehwal-on-PV-Sindhu-Cant-be-friends-with-foes/articleshow/29631341.cms

[56]https://www.sportskeeda.com/badminton/pbl-2018-saina-nehwal-and-i-share-a-hi-bye-relationship-says-pv-sindhu

that of being a thorough professional. Irrespective of her competition, she always means business. Whether it is Sindhu or Li Xuerui, her commitment on court is always 100 per cent.

LEARNING TIP

Professionalism demands that you give your best, irrespective of who your opponent is.

Professionalism is an important value that should be imbibed by all aspiring professionals since it is valued in every shape, size and form. It is very important for the organization to ensure that everyone is working towards the common organizational goal which can be achieved efficiently if the teams are professional enough. It is a bare minimum.

In the game of badminton, the chance to take revenge on an opponent comes often. Players know that with a packed international schedule the possibility of them playing against the same opponent again is very high. But Saina strives to have the maximum impact the very first time. For her, winning over her opponents is important. It is all about the mindset, she likes to win and prefers doing it clinically. Chinese players have traditionally been her favourite opponents and, incidentally, she also has many titles in her name for winning against them.

Saina's Evolution As a Player

From being a diligent student to a confident world-class player, Saina in her professional journey has come a long way. An activity that was used as a way to keep a ten-year-old Saina busy through her summer vacations has metamorphosed into giving India one of its biggest sports icons.

The first stage of her badminton career was when she stepped under the guidance of Nani Prasad and S.M. Arif. During this phase, she learnt more about the art of wielding a racquet and started working on her fitness levels. This time is also significant with her gaining reputation as a player in domestic circuits and foraying into international circuits.

Stage two of Saina's career was when Gopichand retired and opened the Pullela Gopichand Badminton Academy in Hyderabad. Post his victory in the All England Open Badminton Championship in 2001, all the aspiring badminton players in India looked up to him and Saina was no different. With a dream to achieve what Gopichand did in the All England Open Badminton Championship and a desire to learn from his experience she enrolled in Gopichand's Academy. A wise decision, it did not take much time for Gopichand to realize Saina's potential and he started grooming her for the big stage.

This was the phase when the focus moved from building Saina's strength to building her game. She was always hungry for victory, willing to go the distance. All Gopichand did was to provide her with adequate artillery to achieve the vision.

This phase can also be highlighted as the time when Saina was dominating the domestic circuit, winning games at will and showing sparks of being a talent to be reckoned with even in international arena.

Stage three can easily be classified as the period from 2007–08, when Saina started participating in international tournaments on a regular basis. This was still her early phase in the international circuit, where she was beginning to get comfortable with strenuous international schedules and improving on her stamina levels. After facing a few challenges in the initial couple of years, soon Saina took the badminton world by storm by winning three to four titles on a yearly basis.

Stage four was the difficult part of Saina's career when she was troubled with her injuries. But after a lean phase of six to seven months, she pulled herself together to prepare for the ultimate glory of the Olympic medal in 2012. This phase is also marked with her decision to change her coach.

Stage five is the golden part of Saina's career until now. This is when she became the world no. 1 and won two medals back to back in the World Championships.

Saina's life has come a full circle, from being a girl who was inspired by a champion like Pullela Gopichand to moving many country miles ahead to take on the mantle of inspiring her nation to achieve sporting greatness.

Simplicity At Its Best

Saina is a very focused and dedicated individual; it is very rare that anything which is not related to badminton takes precedence for her. Her life in many ways is limited from home to the court and back. Regimented by strict schedules and restricted diets, her conduct is as good as penance.

Her meteoric rise in badminton has kept her devoid of a regular life of fun and friends. But, she understands the price she has to pay for her dreams. In her own words:[57]

> I stay at home because I have no friends. That makes me feel sad, but that's okay. I console myself by thinking, why have friends when I don't have the time for them.

Her day starts early with practice sessions and after a gap of four hours she starts training again. Sundays are usually for rest and she likes spending time with her family, indulging in activities which any normal family does. She avoids going out—to evade unnecessary inconvenience caused to the gentry around. For her, watching movies on television and eating aloo parathas made by her mother is a day well-spent.[58]

A family-oriented person, Saina draws her strength and immense support from her family. Whenever she has been clouded by controversies, her family has stood by her like a

---

[57]http://www.facenfacts.com/NewsDetails/316/why-saina-is-a-great-hope-for-indian-sports.htm

[58]http://www.facenfacts.com/NewsDetails/316/why-saina-is-a-great-hope-for-indian-sports.htm

rock. They do not believe in being over-protective with her, but are just a call away when needed.

From being a nine-year-old enthusiastic child to becoming the national treasure of India, she has come a long way. However, Saina is aware that it won't stay this way for the rest of her life. Retirement and 'hanging the boots' are the harsh realities of any sports personality's life, but she is not affected by it and is in fact very clear about what she wants to do once she retires. A strong advocate of an organized programme to nurture future stars of badminton, she wants to see a well laid out plan for badminton players in India where in the near future the country also has a reserve of eight to ten players to represent it.

She plans to open an academy in northern India, most likely in her home state of Haryana and develop regimented programmes to spot and provide avenues for aspiring talent to grow and do the nation proud someday.

Saina has set a high bar for the generations to come. It would need more than just efforts for someone to claim the space created by her. Her name not only represents women in sports, but has also become a symbol of women empowerment and celebration of womanhood in India, by extension. For every professional, Saina has a fair bit of inspiration to offer. Her career teaches us the importance of dreaming big and working hard at achieving it. When it came to making some of the biggest decisions of her life, she listened to her heart over the voices around; and the rest is for the world to see.

Acknowledgements

As said in the book: 'It takes a village to raise a child,' I consider this book no different. Result of a sacrifice by many, this book will not be complete without acknowledging them.

Harika, my wife, I am sorry for being selfish—this book would have been only a dream without you selflessly supporting me.

Shambhu Sahu my chief editor, this book would have remained a mere concept had you not shown me the way forward. Your support and guidance was more like a friend's then a chief editor.

Tanima Saha, my copy editor, thanks a lot for working with me on developing this book into a fine jewel worth a read, I appreciate all your patience with me.

My kids Dheeish and Naamyaa, thanks for just being there, your presence in my life has inspired me to be the superhuman I always fantasized about.

Last but not the least my parents and family for encouraging my decision to write a book. A lot of this book is a reflection of your upbringing.